MW01234689

COMEBACK

COMEBACK

ALEX AND PHYLLIS LAPERCHIA

Archway Publishing books may be ordered through booksellers or by contacting:

Archway Publishing
1663 Liberty Drive
Bloomington, IN 47403
www.archwaypublishing.com
844-669-3957

Because of the dynamic nature of the Internet, any web addresses or
links contained in this book may have changed since publication and
may no longer be valid. The views expressed in this work are solely those
of the author and do not necessarily reflect the views of the publisher,
and the publisher hereby disclaims any responsibility for them.

Any people depicted in stock imagery provided by Getty Images are
models, and such images are being used for illustrative purposes only.
Certain stock imagery © Getty Images.

Unless otherwise indicated, all Scripture taken from
the Douay–Rheims version of the Bible.

Scripture marked Aramaic Peshitta taken from the Holy Bible from the
Ancient Eastern Text from the Aramaic of the Peshitta translated by
George Lamsa, © 1933 by A. J. Holman Co, All rights reserved.

ISBN: 978-1-6657-2348-0 (sc)
ISBN: 978-1-6657-2346-6 (hc)
ISBN: 978-1-6657-2347-3 (e)

Library of Congress Control Number: 2022908467

Print information available on the last page.

Archway Publishing rev. date: 7/8/2022

To my beloved wife, Phyllis, who is the author of chapter 2. Therefore, we are coauthors of *Comeback*.

Phyllis has a keen interest in politics. She was the president and treasurer of the board of directors of our co-op in New York City, and she is the vice president of our board of directors for our condominium in Florida. I believe that Phyllis has done a creditable job.

Former president of the United States, Donald Trump.
Former First Lady of the United States, Melania Trump.

These remarkable persons may be future president and first lady of the United States. Who knows? What I do know is that Donald Trump never took a cent of his salary in four years as president. He donated $1 million to the victims of Hurricane Harvey. What I do know is that Donald Trump was not a career politician but a successful businessman who became a humanitarian president.

My wife, Phyllis, has a personal story that relates to Donald Trump. When she was a teenager, her parents moved from New Jersey to Jamaica Estates in Queens, New York, where Fred Trump had just constructed an apartment building. It was a luxury building right around the corner, where the Trumps resided in a mansion. Fred Trump often inspected the apartment building to make sure everything was in order. One day, he met Phyllis and her parents. They all became friends. Sometimes Donald Trump would accompany his father. Phyllis had a cousin, David, who was visiting them. He encountered Donald and was invited to the Trump home to play with Donald. They became friends. Donald went on to become a businessman and president, and David became a foot doctor and a businessman.

CONTENTS

PREFACE

I believe the 2020 elections for the rightful president, Donald Trump, as well as the senatorial elections, especially in Georgia, were stolen from the Republicans by the Democrats through widespread election voter fraud.

The Democrats, using the pretext of the COVID-19 virus, changed election laws during state elections while the elections were in progress, especially in Pennsylvania, in clear violation of their states' constitutions. These elections were rife with fraud by election harvesting, counting ballots without verifying signatures, counting ballots of those who were not living in the states and dead people in cemeteries. Ballots were being counted even after the elections were over for days on end. Mail-in ballots flooded the polls because the ballots did not register voters who were Republican. Thus, the Democrats seized the presidency and Senate. They now control all three branches of government.

Through executive orders issued by Joe Biden without the consent of Congress, the oil, shale, and coal industries have been destroyed in this country. Under Trump, we were an oil-exporting producer; now we lag behind Saudi Arabia and Russia, and we are importing oil. The price of oil has doubled from thirty dollars a barrel to sixty-five dollars a barrel and continues to soar. Gasoline prices were stabilized at two dollars a gallon under Trump; they are expected to be five dollars per gallon at year-end.

Carbon taxes, wealth taxes, and higher income taxes will be imposed on all Americans by the Biden administration. They expect the loss of jobs in fossil fuel to be offset by the creation of alternative energy source—namely, wind turbines and solar panels.

The Green New Deal will cost taxpayers an estimated $50 trillion over the next decade. In the meantime, by rejoining the Paris Climate Treaty, China and India are exempt from cutting carbon emissions at all for the next decade. So much for climate change! It's a farce.

Open borders with Mexico will allow illegal immigration to run rampant. These undocumented people, including drug and human traffickers, will be granted amnesty and allowed to vote. Even violent criminals will not be allowed to be deported.

The Democrats plan to make Washington, DC, into a state, thus adding two more Democrats into the Senate. The goal of the left-wing Democrats is to crush the religious Right Republicans and develop the United States into a socialist, perhaps Communist country, in which government controls every aspect of the people's lives. Democracy, dissent, freedom of religion, and the right to assemble and bear arms will be abolished. The government will become a tyrant as it was in the former Soviet Union and is today under Communist China. The Democrats are being financed by the former Nazi collaborator billionaire George Soros and liberal Silicon high-tech billionaires who don't want their corporations broken up with antitrust laws. They are keeping the stock and bond markets from collapsing.

If the Republicans don't take control of the House and the Senate in 2022, our country is doomed. Americans, Democrats and Republicans, wake up before it's too late!

★ x ★

COMEBACK IS DIVIDED INTO FIVE CHAPTERS

Chapter 1 concentrates on organizations that help Republicans win elections through private donations, such as Friends of Zion Center for Diplomacy, a coalition of Jews and Gentiles to promote peace, founded by Dr. Mike Evans.

Chapter 2, "What's It All about? I Want My Country Back!" This chapter addresses several topics of concern today: 1) COVID; 2) immigration; 3) Afghanistan; 4) education; 5) Democrats versus Republicans, which delineates the stark difference between Democrats and Republicans. The Democrats are endeavoring to make our capitalistic democracy into a socialist, tyrannical regime. They now control the three branches of government and must be defeated in 2022. The Republicans need to take back the House and the Senate.

Chapter 3, "The Champion of Freedom of Religion," describes Donald Trump as the antithesis of the Democrats who want to suppress religious freedom and destroy our constitution.

Chapter 4, "China Will Rule the World" details how China wants to replace the US as the world's greatest economy and military power.

Chapter 5, "The Holy Bible, Douay–Rheims" demonstrates the scripture's relevance to Donald Trump. The Holy Bible from the Ancient Eastern Text translates "Gog" to "China." Also, "and I will send a fire on the people who dwell peacefully in the islands, Japan." China will devastate Japan with nuclear weapons in 2043 in revenge for the Rape of Nanking during WWII. The Holy Bible from the Ancient Eastern Text (Ezekiel 39:6) corresponds exactly with Cracking the Apocalypse Code by Gerard Bodson, which confirms that China will indeed attack Japan with nuclear weapons in 2043.

Nota bene: All scriptural quotations are taken from the Douay–Rheims Bible by Rev. George Leo Haydock; there are a few scriptural quotations taken from the Holy Bible from the Ancient Eastern Text from the Aramaic of the Peshitta translated by George Lamsa using the word "China." The Douay–Rheims Bible is a Catholic Bible in public domain. The Holy Bible from the Ancient Eastern Text uses "China," while the Douay–Rheims Bible uses the word "Gog." The Hebrew word "Gog" means "eastern tribes." The Aramaic Peshitta identifies these eastern tribes as China. Examples: Isaiah 23:12; Ezekiel 38:1, 2; Ezekiel 38:14; Ezekiel 38:18; Ezekiel 39:11; Daniel 11:30; and Revelation 20:18.

ACKNOWLEDGMENTS

I have known my wife, Phyllis, for fifty-four years.

I have known my godson, Viani, for seventeen years.

These very intelligent people provided me with much of the data and statistics included in my book. Also, Phyllis is my constant caregiver since my affliction with Parkinson's disease.

Alison Schaible, the owner of Perfecta Transcription, has done an excellent typing job of my original manuscript. I write in longhand, my penmanship is poor, and Alison is a terrific typist. She is familiar with book editing and handwritten terminology.

The Association of Mature American Citizens (*AMAC* magazine) has granted permission to the authors to reprint articles from their magazines in our book *Comeback*, published by Archway Publishers, an affiliate of Simon and Schuster.

In the words of Rebecca Weber, chief executive officer and editor in chief of *AMAC* magazine, "Let us all pray for the youngest generation among us, pray they should live a life of freedom and prosperity, unhindered and free of the radical teachings of the dangerous, socialists, liberal left who roam in places of high power and government. I am reminded of a prayer my grandfather once said over me. His prayer: That all of his grandchildren would be shielded from the horrors of war, and that our nation would endure because of the bravest men and women who fought and died to keep us free."

A special thanks goes to Elizabeth Timm and Pam Smith of AMAC for assisting in making it possible to include the thirteen articles.

OTHER BOOKS AND WRITINGS BY ALEX AND PHYLLIS LAPERCHIA

Alex LaPerchia

My Favorite Bible Quotations, Newman Springs Publishing, 2018

Food for the Soul, University Press of America, 2015

Satan and the Saint, Sterling House Publisher Inc., 1999

A New York City Teacher Learns Love, Magnificat Press, 1991

All God's Children, Libra Publishers, 1987

A Spiritual Guide to Eternal Life, Philosophical Library, 1977

Phyllis LaPerchia

"Behavioral Disorders, Learning Disabilities and Megavitamin Therapy", Adolescence, Vol. XXII, No.87, Fall 1987, Libra Publishers, Inc.

The Maiden Who Turned into a Violet (work in progress)

The Third Person and Other Memoirs (work in progress)

CHAPTER ONE
Why Is Trump a Champion?

TRUMP IS TRULY A CHAMP TO SEVENTY-FIVE million Americans, including me. But he is an antihero to a similar number of Americans, perhaps more but probably less. I make this assumption based on the huge number of people he drew to his rallies. Where were Biden's rallies? Indeed, he had a precious few rallies, and a precious few people attended them.

I suspect this career politician was elected president not because he enjoyed a remarkable career (?) of thirty-six years as a senator in Delaware and eight brilliant years (?) as vice president under Obama. Rhode Island is the tiniest state in the US; Delaware is the second smallest state. Biden was elected by Trump haters who preferred a swamp creature who represents the status quo.

Old people, like me, want to live out their lives the way we have lived them for the past sixty, seventy, or eighty years. On the other hand, young people are idealistic liberals who want to destroy what they perceive to be a corrupt system stacked against them.

Liberalism is not sinful. Since the beginning of recorded history, the common people were ruled by absolute monarchs who reigned in luxury, with cruelty over an impoverished populace. The Bill of Rights enshrined our right to be governed by the consent of the public, except for slaves. Shamefully, the grievous sin of black slavery was not abolished until 1865 by the Republican president Abraham Lincoln.

The young people think they have plenty of years ahead of them. Old people like me, seventy-nine years old, know that our days are numbered. We are satisfied, middle-class people—not rich or poor. We deem our lives successful, and for most of us, life has been good, and we are content with the portion God has dealt us.

Permit me to digress with some personal history. I have been married to my beloved wife, Phyllis, for fifty-two years. She wanted children, but I did not. Why not? Because I did not have what it takes to be a good father. Believe it or not, I was certain that I could not bear the stress of being a good parent in our chaotic world.

Truth be told, I confessed to a Catholic priest before marriage, and he told me I did not trust God. I told him that I did not have the mental stability to raise a family in this chaotic world. He responded that I should trust God to give me the strength to do so. He refused to give me absolution for the grave sin of having sex with my future wife without being open to new life. Actually, this is what inspired me to write *A Spiritual Guide to Eternal Life*, in which I defended my position. Following is an extract from this book:

> There is an exiguous but growing minority of married couples who have chosen not to have children. (20% today) We simply cannot cope with the enormous pressure of raising a family in today's

society. I honestly don't believe it is selfishness but survival that impels us not to have children. We are almost overcome by the frantic world we live in and can barely sustain ourselves. It is far better that we remain childless than to become unfit parents.

We do not get off lightly. In old age who will want to be with us? My nieces and nephews have their own parents to look after. Will strangers in nursing homes worry about us? We do not look forward to the elderly years. I believe it is the duty of married couples who don't have children to dedicate themselves to good works and charity. We have the time and resources. Only through altruism may we trust in the forgiveness and mercy of God.

As a Catholic, I share the sentiments of Joseph Gallagher CSP, a priest, in his catechism *To Be a Catholic*, which bears the imprimatur (an official declaration that a book is free from doctrinal and moral error). Concerning a married couples' responsibility for new life, he asserts: "Each couple must determine in the light of all circumstances of their married life what is the unique creative partnership God invites them to share with Him." In regard to how a Catholic couple should plan their family, he writes: "Through a conscientious assessment of what they should do to future the good of their family and of society. In this assessment, they are helped by the teaching of the church, their own family situation, and the examples of other faithful Christians. As in all life decisions here too people finally decide according to a well-formed Christian conscience."

As for my book, I also received the imprimatur from a Catholic bishop in 1977 and proudly retain this document of church approval.

My wife and I are retired educators. She was a New York City public junior high principal with more than two thousand students, and I was a New York City public high school English teacher. We loved serving our students and have no regrets about our careers, although our jobs were not easy. Our disadvantaged students (they lived in high-crime and impoverished school districts) showed us much love even though their own lives were often difficult. In fact, I published a book about my school experiences titled *A New York City Teacher Learns Love*.

Phyllis and I were coworkers with the Missionaries of Charity founded by Saint Mother Teresa. Saint Mother Teresa's religious order is strong and growing. We were privileged to meet Saint Mother Teresa one day. What a blessed memory! Phyllis counseled homeless women in a convent, while I gave them Bible studies. For six years, I had a street ministry in New York City.

Recently, I read an autobiography by Mike Evans titled *The Great Awakening Is Coming*. Mike Evans predicts a religious revival soon to take place in America and around the world. Mike's mother was Jewish; therefore, he is considered Jewish in Judaism. Mike's father was an alcoholic Catholic who would beat his wife and son. Mike's mother died when he was a child. He was placed in foster homes; some people were kind, while others were abusive to him. He doesn't disclose if he was physically or sexually abused. We tend to forget childhood traumas even though they remain in our subconscious.

When Mike was eleven years old, Jesus appeared to him. Mike then determined he would preach the Gospel of Jesus Christ written by the apostles. He joined the military at seventeen, attending a Bible college after his stint in the military. Mike studied and preached the Word while remaining nondenominational. His Jewish heritage made him attractive to the evangelicals since they consider Jews to be the elect of God. He preached in many

Protestant churches; many had good male pastors, while others had adulterers, addicts of pornography, and hypocrites.

Meantime, Mike traveled the world preaching that Christ died to redeem all people. Mike would preach to people of every religion who would listen to him. Jesus commanded his disciples to travel to the ends of the earth, seeking to baptize people in the name of the Father, the Son, and the Holy Spirit.

Mike had inner locutions when Jesus spoke to his heart. One time, he preached to forty thousand Hindus. The Holy Spirit prompted Mike to discard his planned sermon and deliver this simple message. Thrice, Mike spoke the two words "See Jesus" and sat down. The crowd was bewildered but stayed silent. Then a Hindu doctor ran up to the microphone, crying, and shouted to the stunned audience that he was the director of a school for the blind.

He related that three girls who were blind from birth were able to see when they heard the words "See Jesus." Of course, the news was reported throughout the Indian media, and a hundred thousand people filled a stadium to hear Mike's next sermon, which he delivered in English and was translated into Hindu.

Another time, Mike wanted to preach a sermon to Buddhists, but the stadium was empty. Mike prayed on his knees for an hour for people to show up. Then people started to trickle into the stadium. Before he knew it, the stadium was packed. This took place in a former Communist country called Cambodia, where the atheist Khmer Rouge had murdered two million innocent people under the Communist dictator Pol Pot. They were killed in open fields and villages until his death in an uprising.

Back in the United States, Mike and his wife drove across Texas to visit a young man who had been crushed in an auto accident. His heart and lungs were severely damaged. Mike prayed over the young man and told him he was loved by God. The machines started whizzing, and doctors and nurses rushed into the intensive care unit. After hours of evaluation, a tearful nurse announced to Mike and his wife that the young man was completely healed. God performed a mighty miracle through Mike.

All I can say with complete conviction is that God is using Mike in a very powerful way. I believe in the power of prayer. If people pray in earnest, God will answer their prayers, even perform miracles. Today, Mike lives in Israel, the home of his ancestors. He continues to preach the Gospels of Jesus in a ministry stretching across the globe.

Dr. Mike Evans has not forgotten that his mother was Jewish and his father was Christian. He established a coalition of Jews and Christians to promote peace between Jews and Gentiles, named the Friends of Zion Center for Diplomacy. These are his words in his global magazine, "Friends of Zion," (February 2021): "I am thrilled to tell you that the kitchen project at your Friends of Zion Center is complete. This is such a wonderful facility and it will allow us to do so much more to meet the needs of 'The least of these,' especially the poor holocaust survivors. Together we are shining a bright light of Christian love all across the nation of Israel."

What a joy it is to me to have read this book and realize that there are such good people in the world. I know there is an evil system in the world set up by evil people. However, we can be joyful to know that when Jesus returns to earth, He will dispel all evil; He will cast all the evildoers and their evil ones into hell during the millennium. Good people should rejoice every day because we have faith that all will be well, and all manner of things will be well, as Blessed Julian of Norwich has prophesied.

My wife, Phyllis, and I are members of the Faith and Freedom Coalition founded by Dr. Ralph Reed. This organization is giving Christians a voice in government with two million members and supporters.

We believe that the leftist Democrats are willing to do anything to win elections and seize government power. We believe the evidence is overwhelming that the 2020 election was stolen due to voter fraud. The Democrats now have control of the Senate (Democrats have fifty seats, and Republicans have fifty seats, but Vice President Kamala Harris may cast the tie-breaking vote). If the Democrats keep their majority in the House, they will have complete control of the federal government.

They have pledged they will reward themselves with four left-ist Senators by making Puerto Rico and the District of Columbia into states. Second, they will expand the number of seats on the Supreme Court and pack these seats with radical leftists, thus giving the Left a permanent majority on the Supreme Court. Third, they will open the floodgates to more migration from Central America and Mexico, thus creating for themselves tens of millions of new voters for socialism. Conservative voters will never win the presidency again.

We must win control of Congress in 2022 and the president in 2024! Donald Trump has commended the Faith and Freedom Coalition with high praise. He declared in writing that the organization with its leadership, Ralph and JoAnne Reed, has given him incredible support, and he is grateful for their commitment to their shared cause. Mike Pence thanked Ralph Reed for playing a pivotal role in marshaling a movement that's made such a difference in the life of our nation. Mark Levin pleaded with the public to help save freedom in America by supporting the Faith and Freedom Coalition. Sean Hannity predicts the Faith and Freedom Coalition is the modern-day Christian Coalition of yesteryear. Other prominent people who support the Faith and Freedom Coalition and Ralph Reed are Newt Gingrich, Senator Marco Rubio, Sarah Palin, and Senator Ted Cruz.

I, personally, have been honored by Dr. Ralph Reed, who wrote the introduction to my book *Satan and the Saint*, a biography of Saint John Vianney, the patron saint of all Catholic parish priests. Dr. Reed was then the executive director of the Christian Coalition at the time of the book's publication in 1999. These are his words:

Through obedience to God, prayer and working together we will be victorious over the evils of the dissolution of families through divorce, the widespread corrosion of values and morals, the horror of abortion, the scourge of drug abuse, the escalation of crime, the glorification of pornography and violence.

Saint John Vianney understood the devil's temptations and attacks through his love of God and fellow man. He personified the gospel message of doing spiritual and corporal works of mercy. His life was a triumph of love and goodness. Through this book, people of all faiths will be uplifted by the life of this wonderful saint and see the relevance of his teachings to their own lives.

As retired educators, my wife and I have an active interest in what is taking place in the public schools in our country. Therefore, we are contributors and supporters of the Foundation of Liberty and American Greatness (FLAG). Nick Adams is the founder and executive director. I would like to share FLAG's school pledge with you:

I declare the world is a better place because of America. We're safer, healthier and wealthier. American exceptionalism has improved our lives. After freedom, inspiration is America's next greatest import. The American dream is the dream of mankind. Without America, terror, tyranny and torture would reign. It's vital to civilization. America isn't perfect, but it's the best idea the world has ever had. Anti-Americanism has no place in our society or world. I'm proud to be a friend of the United States of America.

Already there are two thousand schools across the country that have signed this pledge. This is encouraging to my wife and me. Recently, we received a 2021 Taxpayer Research Opinion Survey on socialist political indoctrination in our schools. The results were shocking. A recent Harris Poll found about 50 percent of American voters aged twenty-three to thirty-eight want the United States to become a socialist country. The results of a recent national survey of millennials are chilling: More than 25 percent say they are not proud to be an American, or patriotic. Thirty-five percent say they are not proud of America's history. Sixty-three percent say America is racist, and 60 percent say America is sexist. Almost 50 percent do not believe America is or will return to be a great country, and 14 percent say it was never great. Almost 50 percent do not believe in American capitalism and the free enterprise system. A few research polls showed that 41 percent who are protesting around the country are age eighteen to twenty-nine, and 38 percent are thirty- to forty-nine-year-old Democrat voters.

These statistics left my wife and me stunned with disbelief. What is happening to our beloved United States? Here are some answers. For years, ultraliberal workers in our public school system have been promoting an anti-American curriculum for college, high school, and even grammar school children.

They have been teaching our nation's children that the US Constitution is a document of oppression and denounces America's melting pot heritage and ideals.

The Foundation for Liberty and American greatness (FLAG) reveals that Obama's Common Core nationalized education program, of which Communist Bill Ayers was a contributor, has been a terrible failure by all accounts in just nine years since it was started. Common Core was instituted without the consent of Congress at a staggering cost to the taxpayer of more than $80 billion. Many teachers and most Americans are not aware of the Left's radical political doctrine by using their power to teach America's children our democracy is racist, sexist, and discriminatory. The radical Left (progressives, socialists, and Communists) have the power to hire and fire our nation's teachers and to deny jobs, pay raises, and promotions to those who fail to tow their radical political line.

My wife, Phyllis, and I are retired educators. We are heartbroken. We see how the public education system is being destroyed before our very eyes. We pity the vulnerable students in our country who are subject to this poisonous brainwashing. We must make every effort to oust left-wing politicians and teachers from their insidious plans and actions. God help us in this battle for the souls of our young people.

My wife, Phyllis, and I support Judicial Watch, a nonpartisan, government watchdog organization founded by Tom Fitton, dedicated to exposing government corruption and abuse. He and his team have filed more than sixty-five lawsuits that are forcing the release of government records levied against Donald Trump to destroy his presidency. The motto of Judicial Watch is "No one is above the law." The team at Judicial Watch continues to lead the fight against the Washington establishment, otherwise called the swamp. They continue to lead the fight for honest elections through massive voter roll cleaning.

Every vote should be legal. They are currently suing Colorado, North Carolina, Illinois, and Pennsylvania for not following federal election law. Judicial Watch has a lawsuit against San Francisco's illegal and deadly sanctuary policy, which is scheduled to go on trial this April. They seek to enforce immigration policy throughout the country.

Judicial Watch wants to hold the Biden administration accountable for the facts about Biden's family influence–peddling schemes in Ukraine and China. On Election Day, Donald Trump had the votes to win the presidency. These vote totals were changed after Election Day, giving Joe Biden the margin of victory in swing states. There is strong evidence that the battleground states' laws were violated in the handling and counting of mail-in ballots. It is clear that had only those votes arriving in the counting rooms and tallied on Election Day been allowed to count, Donald Trump would have been the unchallenged winner.

In his book *A Republic Under Assault*, the *New York Times* best-selling author Tom Fitton delineates documents showing how the Democratic National Committee and senior Obama administration officials, including Barack Obama, paid for and used the Steele dossier, filled with Russian disinformation, to lie to the FISA court in order to spy on the Trump presidential campaign and President Trump. These and more dirty secrets of Obamagate and the impeachment coup attack are exposed. The book shows how Soros-funded groups attack states that seek to protect legitimate elections by challenging voter ID laws and how the Left is promoting mail-in voting, which could increase vote fraud and election chaos. The book underscores how illegal sanctuary policies are exploited across America and how our nation's sovereignty has been under assault by radical open-border advocates.

Our founding documents acknowledge that the United States must have clearly defined and protected borders. A country without borders is no country at all!

TV host Sean Hannity declares *A Republic Under Assault: The Left's Ongoing Attack on American Freedom* is a must-read for every American who wants to save our nation. I can add no further recommendation for reading this book than this erudite author of *Live Free or Die*.

Hot off the press is *Socialists Don't Sleep: Christians Must Rise or America Will Fall* by Cheryl Chumley. This book was just published by Humanix Press and has a 2021 copyright. The book jacket proffers an incisive insight into the book's content:

> In this blunt assessment of the deep danger America is facing from the left, award-winning journalist, Washington Times columnist, and bestselling author, Cheryl Chumley, exposes all the sneaky ways the secular left has pressed socialism into

American politics and life—and why Christians are the only ones who can stop it. At stake are the freedoms Americans cherish, unless we act now. The great hope for this nation lies in going back to the founding principles of Judeo-Christian principles.

In this book, Cheryl takes you through all the ways that Democrats and the radical Left are planting dangerous seeds of socialist principles into our everyday life, including public schools that teach America is not exceptional; politicians who support entitlement and not hard work to get elected; and a generation raised without God or a god that can be whatever is wished at the time.

It's through God that we can reel back the entitlement mind-set and get insight into a government that humbly, honestly, and properly serves rather than regulates and rules. Only then can socialism in America be defeated. *Socialists Don't Sleep* lays out the problems and then offers clear guidance for both short- and long-term solutions to rid the country of socialism with a small *s*—before it turns into widespread Socialism with a capital S.

In Cheryl Chumley's own words, "If America is to be free, America needs Christians to get louder."

CHAPTER TWO
What's It All About? I Want My Country Back!

COVID

WHEN I WAS A LITTLE GIRL, AROUND TEN years old, I was sitting on our front porch in a small town in South Jersey, Penns Grove, with my dad, watching Fourth of July fireworks. My father turned to me and said, "Phyllis, remember my words: we will not be destroyed by an atomic bomb but by germ warfare!"

When we first learned about the COVID-19 breakout, I said to myself, "Boy, was my father right!" And I immediately thought this was not just an accident but planned. And to this day, I believe that! More and more evidence points in that direction. I personally can't prove it, but it is very interesting that in the fall of 2019, the military world games competition was hosted by China to bring unity and peace, and the COVID-19 pandemic happened shortly after that. I also believe there were cases already in existence before we officially knew of this virus, and several people were already exposed to it through these games. Already there were cases not reported. But China knew and never warned us, and we may have known as well! And ironically, the great Dr. Fauci helped fund the research at the Wuhan Lab but denied it till recently. They were experimenting on whether mice would become more ill from the virus than the bats. Could it have leaked from the lab accidently? Sure! Or could it have been done on purpose? Probably! Very interesting that it happened right after the Chinese-sponsored military world games! Could this have been done to affect the 2020 election to destroy President Donald Trump? Again, probably!

And during this time, President Donald Trump pushed for a vaccine to fight this pandemic but also kept suggesting to have therapy and treatments for those patients who already had the virus.

Where was the great Dr. Fauci to recommend this or work with the president to make it happen? Trump believed in hydroxychloroquine, and people made fun of him and mocked him, but now we know it works. A lot of lives could have been saved! Today we can take Regeneron's monoclonal antibody cocktail/therapy, and immediately within the first three days after coming down with the COVID-19 virus, you will get better much faster. Vaccines need much more testing long-term to see what could happen years after receiving the vaccines or immediately. A woman I knew, who was about thirty-three, got the vaccine and a week later died from blood clots in her heart. I personally am allergic to glycerin, and that is a preservative used to preserve the vaccines, so I cannot take the vaccine.

The COVID vaccine came out in less than a year. Most vaccines take a minimum or four years to be developed and tested. I understand there was an emergency, but people should have been warned that it was risky to take something that hasn't been totally tested and researched, and moving forward, if there are enough people who have a bad reaction, there should warnings about the side effects of the vaccine. If enough deaths from the vaccine occur, it should be removed till perfected. Although I realize that it was in an emergency pandemic that the vaccines were developed, I do not believe that if enough people get very sick or die, it should be continued, and I do not believe that this should be forced on young children who can develop their own immune systems. Case in point, I interviewed several young people between the ages of eighteen and twenty-five who had the COVID virus, and they all said it was like a two- to three-day cold. Nothing extreme. And then they develop their own immune system.

And except for very ill children with other conditions, why would we introduce something foreign and not experimented on enough to twelve-year-olds and younger children? I understand giving it to most of the elderly who are in a more compromised health position, as well as younger people with special conditions.

But one size fits all does not work here. President Biden's mandates that *all* workers be forced to take it and all school-aged children be forced to take it can be dangerous. Most medicines that have enough people who get adverse reactions have strong warnings on the packages, and if even a few people die from it, it is removed from the shelves. And enough have had the above, and now we are learning that the vaccine loses its effectiveness well before a year, and now you must take a booster. Recent research was done on the J&J vaccine (*Epoch Times*, November 8–9, 2021, US edition). Researchers with the Mayo Clinic compared blood-clotting data from Olmstead County, Minnesota, between 2001 and 2015 to data on blood clotting with those who received the Johnson and Johnson shot. Those who got the J&J shot were 3.5 times more likely to develop cerebral venous sinus thrombosis than the general population during that time period.

So, dear President Biden, one size does not fit all, and some people could actually die with your mandate. It is about the science! And would you trust the NIH, headed by Dr. Fauci, who until recently denied his involvement with the Wuhan Lab research and finally broke down and admitted it (under the pressure of Senator Rand Paul)? The virus leaked out of the lab either by accident or on purpose. We will never know!

And would you trust a man, Dr. Fauci, who allegedly has done dog experiments on healthy beagles that are cruel and painful and cause death? The beagles in one of the experiments were injected and force-fed with an experimental drug for several weeks before killing and dissecting them! Another experiment Dr. Fauci funded involved young, healthy beagles where they were eaten alive by parasite-infected flies. This smacks of animal abuse, and charges should be filed against the great Dr. Fauci. And one last experiment Dr. Fauci is allegedly responsible for: experiments on AIDS orphans in NYC.

The experiments were approved by the NIH. These orphans were used as lab rats in deadly AIDS drug trials. The drug tests were fatal for many children, and others suffered greatly during the experiments. This smacks of child abuse, and the evil Dr. Fauci should be brought on child abuse charges and suffer the consequences!

Remember, President Trump never trusted Dr. Fauci, and boy was he more than right! But President Biden lauds him and follows things that make no scientific sense!

Immigration

My family immigrated to America at the turn of the century, the early 1900s. My mother's side were from Odessa, Russia, and her father was from Austria. There was a pogrom going on in Russia, and a wealthy baron got them out of Russia and set up a small town in South Jersey. It consisted of mostly chicken farms, but there was a rubber factory in the town as well. My grandfather on my mother's side ran the rubber factory in this beautiful town of Woodbine, New Jersey, with the most majestic trees and best chickens and tomatoes and corn. It was just a few miles from the Jersey Shore, where I spent many of my summers when I was growing up. My grandfather on my father's side owned a small store with many items, but as time progressed, he sold appliances and other household items. They came here under very tough circumstances but gained their freedom and worked hard.

My husband, Alex's, family were of Italian descent. His father was born in the small town of Matera, where they lived in caves. They were very poor; at a very young age (about fourteen), he was asked by his father to find work in northern Italy during WWI, as he was the oldest child, and they told him they could not afford to keep him. So, my father-in-law ventured to north Italy and built the coffins for the soldiers who died in the war. A few years later at about nineteen years old, he and a cousin wanted to move to America. They were sponsored by a cousin who already lived in America. They came to America by ship and traveled in very unhealthy conditions. Many became very ill during the journey, and a few died. My father-in-law first started out as a worker but saved his money and bought property and opened a bakery shop. The Depression wiped out all his money, and he lost all his property. His bakery he lost to another local bakery because of what they used to call the Black Hand, which was the Mafia.

But he still found work and was sent to Washington, DC, during the Depression. He then spent the rest of his life as a house painter. My mother-in-law worked in a factory as a seamstress.

To come to America was their dream, and they could definitely enjoy a better life here. They worked hard and made their own money and never expected for this great country to give them handouts. They respected America and always praised this great land. Future generations joined the navy and the marines and gave back to this country and fought to protect this great land and preserve not only our freedom but the freedom of many other countries as well!

My uncle Sonny was one of those soldiers during WWII. While in Germany and flying a plane, he and his partner were shot down into German farmland. The Germans captured him and took him to the German prisoners of war camp. His partner died in his arms. While staying in the prisoner of war camp, he was approached by the head of the camp. He asked my uncle if his last name was Alexenburg. And he responded yes! The head of the camp went on to ask him if Sam Alexenburg was his father, and again he responded yes. The head of the camp then said that during peacetime, he visited the rubber factory in Woodbine, New Jersey, and he met my grandfather, and he was very grateful that my grandfather helped him to learn about the rubber factory. He then told my uncle that he would save him, and he would make sure he was taken care of while in the prison.

Comparing the old immigration policies with what is going on today, immigration was done in an orderly fashion. America opened her arms to many people and nationalities but with a sense of order. Nobody crossed borders illegally! There was a system of things.

But today, especially under the Biden administration, there is complete chaos! And because of this lack of planning, it is making conditions much worse for our country and the immigrants as well.

I am so nauseous! I am really upset, and I feel for those kids they're using! Our country, but more specifically the Biden administration, should be ashamed of using immigrants for votes and power and not caring how they are going to eat and have shelter. The powers that be are just using them for their own power. Not one of those politicians have even visited to see the horrendous conditions these immigrants are living in. Our president and vice president and the Speaker of the House do not really care about these poor immigrants and about you and me. They only care about their own power. It is such a sad situation. Not even testing for COVID and protecting our country and the immigrants. Yet mandating that business workers and hospital workers and schools must be vaccinated! Hypocrisy! Pure hypocrisy!

We must care for those less fortunate than ourselves but in an organized and legal manner where all will benefit! There must be better conditions created where people really care! Not even showing up to show that they care—Mr. President, Ms. Vice President, and Ms. Speaker of the House!

And now President Biden is sneaking in immigrants to different states in the middle of the night, and airplanes and buses are transporting them there. Again, there is no planning with states through the governors and their agencies. And because these immigrants are not checked for COVID and other diseases, we are all at risk!

In addition to all this, terrorist and criminals are sneaking through to our country as well with the open borders. Just recently in the state of Florida, one of these illegal immigrants, living with a family, shot and killed the father of four children in the house he was staying in.

What about the human trafficking that has increased in the United States since the open borders—and not to mention an increase in the buying and selling of drugs since President Biden opened up the borders. Are you happy now, President Biden and Vice President Harris and Speaker of the House, Ms. Nancy Pelosi?

And recently, the Supreme Court ruled that you were to go back to Trump's "Stay in Mexico," yet you are defying these orders and allowing thousands of new immigrants to trash our border! Just ignoring the Supreme Court decision. You are not protecting your citizens, which is definitely your responsibility as president of the US.

Are you happy you are destroying our country now, President Biden, Vice President Harris, and Speaker of the House Pelosi? My, how you have changed in your political viewpoints, Speaker of the House Ms. Nancy Pelosi and President Biden, since 2005 when I heard your speeches with totally opposite positions on immigration and other areas that will be discussed in future chapters.

Afghanistan

I will never forget 9/11. I was a principal of one of the largest middle schools in NYC. My secretary came running into my office and screamed, "One of the towers at the World Trade Center has fallen!" I called my husband to turn on the news to confirm this. He called back and said, "Yes, it's true," and then the second tower fell. I then received the official word to evacuate the building. Outside the school building, there were hundreds of parents clamoring to pick up their children. I then shifted into gear and organized the outside of the building with all guidance counselors behind tables, according to grade, with a list of students by grade. I assigned security officers to keep the parents in control and calm outside, and others to escort the students one class at a time out of the building, with the assistance of their teacher. When they arrived to our Loggia, the names of students were called out, and parents escorted them out. Thank God all went smoothly, and all students were picked up by a family member.

From the roof of our school, we could see the buildings coming down. It was like something from the Apocalypse. As the day went on, I received phone calls from the families of the teachers and other personnel in the school. Some reported known deaths from the attack, and one call was from a fiancé of one of my teachers to say he was OK but was going into the second building. He was an ex-marine and wanted to help out. He never made it!

And of course, this led up to the war in Iraq (3/2003–2/2011) and war in Afghanistan (10/2001–8/2021). This was the longest war in the history of our country. The war, according to President Trump, was supposed to end May 1, 2021. But President Biden changed the date of the agreement so it would be closer to the anniversary of 9/11. Did this have any effect on the debacle that occurred as we withdrew almost four months later? Probably!

How does a president / commander in chief make a decision to withdraw all of his troops and leave many Americans and the Afghan nationalists behind? There were only thirteen service men—eleven marines, one army, and one navy—left behind to assist in the evacuation. And then our commander in chief / president leaves all our sophisticated machinery behind! What was he thinking? And then he leaves it up to the leaders / the Taliban to decide who leaves and who stays. Thousands of people evacuated, some hanging on to the airplanes as they left, falling to their deaths. But most of those first evacuated were just regular Afghanistan citizens. Many Americans and Afghanistan nationalists were not allowed through!

Where were the attempts from our country to get those remaining out? There were attempts from other countries to get them out. There was a recent attempt by Israel with funding from a wealthy Jewish businessman to get some of those remaining out, and I believe it was a successful mission. These Americans and Afghan nationalists were in a safe house in Afghanistan, and the Taliban found out where they were and were ready to capture them. The plane left just in time. There were attempts by other philanthropists and Christian groups to get them out as well! Some were held up by our government! In addition, I believe there were also attempts by England as well. Where are those remaining Americans and Afghan nationalists now? Not a word from our government! Are they captured and being tortured or killed? Not a word!

In addition to the above, there was a philanthropic Englishman who saved two hundred dogs on a secret flight. Other animal-protection agencies are working through the red tape and helping to get the dogs out.

One of the most serious debacles in this whole mess is that a suicide bomber killed our thirteen soldiers and many citizens! If things were done properly in our withdrawal from Afghanistan, this would never have happened. These soldiers were in the prime of their lives and sacrificed their lives for our country. God Bless them. To lose this war is bad enough, but to withdraw from this war in such a chaotic manner is inexcusable and unacceptable.

And to add salt to the injury, the Taliban are celebrating in their streets with our weapons and our equipment and their music as complete victors!

This event has the world viewing us as no longer a world superpower. And the motto "Nemo Resideo" (No Man Left Behind), which is the motto of the military and all soldiers, did not apply to this situation or the American citizens and the Afghan nationalists left behind. To think of the hell those left behind are going through makes me nauseated. We must care about them, President Biden!

As President Trump said, although he made the agreement with the Taliban, if they deviated with one word, the agreement would be over, and they would know who was boss. You let this happen by mixing up the order of things, withdrawing all the troops before evacuating our Americans and Afghan nationalists who were promised to be helped after siding with America. And again, leaving our military weapons and machines behind! And yet you pride yourself in being successful with this withdrawal. Well, the polls say differently—38 percent and dropping!

Education

Having been an educator for more than thirty-four years, this section is very dear to my heart. I started my career in education because my husband was a teacher, I was an actuary assistant, and I came home much later than he did. He said, "Why don't you become a paraprofessional?" I asked him what a paraprofessional was, and he responded, "An assistant teacher in the classroom." So, he got me the name of a few principals to visit in the South Bronx, which was near the high school where he was an English teacher. I called up one of the principals for an interview. As an aside, I had never heard of the Bronx, having been raised for seventeen years in South Jersey in a town of six thousand residents.

My husband then dropped me off in front of this small elementary school in the South Bronx. I met with the principal, and he explained the program and told me I had to be approved by the community. (I am sure he thought he would never see me again.) So off I went to the Westchester Community Center in the South Bronx. As I was given a number and waiting to be interviewed for the position, I noticed I was the only Caucasian in the room. I remember thinking, *Wow! Now I know how the African American people feel in an all-white world!* Yes, at twenty-one, I was aware of racial differences. But even at that age, I did not choose to see differences. I saw all peoples as part of the family of humanity. And to this day, I feel that way.

My number was called, and I met with an African American woman. I thought, *This will be my last interview, and back I would go to being an actuary assistant in Manhattan.* Boy was I wrong! She told me that it was a program for the community residents to get jobs in the schools, and family income was a factor. Well, my husband, as a teacher in 1969, was only making $5,000 a year but was above the regulations.

However, from my interview, she felt that I would care about these children, and I would be good for the community. So began my educational career, thanks to this wonderful woman.

I then called the principal of the school to let him know I had been accepted and dropped off the paperwork saying so. He assigned me to the math lab federal program because of my background in math. I began my educational career/journey in September 1969.

The math lab program was very interesting. It was to help students who were deficient in math improve. It was to show the relevance of math in their everyday lives. The class was broken into groups. We explored math creatively. I remember going outside and having students measure their shadows in angles. By making curtains for the classroom, they learned measurement and fractions. At the end of the year, the other para and I put on a math lab talent show with a theme in mind, such as the fifties, and the students made decorations out of different geometric shapes. It was all related to math!

According to a federal standardized test, our students improved. Now I am wondering what race differences or "woke" or "CRT" have to do with math. In this program, cultural difference or color differences were not even noticed. I recognized that some students had a better math sense than others. Some of my students who were Latino did not understand a word of English but could figure out math problems because of their math sense.

During the next five years, I got my undergrad degree in elementary education and was looking for a teaching job, but because of the financial problems in New York City, there were only layoffs. So, I was one of the casualties. My math background saved me because there was a shortage of math teachers, so I became a math teacher on the high school level. At the wise advice of our principal, I was told to get along with the students with problems in the school and to get a master's degree in special education.

I listened and then was put into the special education unit as a coordinator and then the assistant principal. I was asked to help start and create a program called the Retail Academy. It was a program for going from school to business. The joint effort was between the high school and Alexander's department store. There was also a store/business that the students ran. It was not a typical school store. It was a business run by the students. It also involved special education and general educations students working together. It was one of the first inclusion programs in NYC. A teacher taught a marketing class related to this program. The students were given positions in the store according to what level they rose to in the program (manager, salesperson, buyer, marketing, etc.), and many of our students got jobs in Alexander's department stores. Several newspapers and news stations throughout the country covered the program.

We even received a congratulations letter from the forty-fifth president of the United States, Donald Trump, before he was president, when he was a businessman. It was prominently displayed on the entrance wall to the store. We also became members of the Bronx Chamber of Commerce. I was named the Bronx supervisor of the year by the superintendent of Bronx high schools and interviewed on CNBC.

Again, the program was about the success of the students and inclusion. It was about looking for the common denominator and everyone receiving good experiences, a good education, and real-life experiences. It was about desiring to succeed, acceptance of our differences, and working together. No one even mentioned or thought about their differences racially or special needs. In fact, the manager of the store was a special needs student. He excelled at running a business. He got a good job after graduating. This shows that capitalism works!

Four years later, I became the principal of the second largest middle school (sixth to eighth grade) in NYC. The school had 2,200 students from fifty-nine countries (mostly Latino from Central and South America; Indians from India, African Americans, Chinese, Russian, Greeks, et al.). I received grants for several programs. The first one I would like to highlight is the Inclusion Program—the first in middle school in the city of New York. The program consisted of monolingual special needs students, monolingual general education students, bilingual special needs students, bilingual general education students. The bilingual component was the first in the country. The classes were mixed with special needs and general education students, and the two teachers (special education teacher and the general education teacher) worked together with the students in one classroom, with an additional paraprofessional assigned to some special education student or just the classroom. It went by subject area. The same was done for the bilingual special education classes and the bilingual general education students.

We also had many after-school programs, including tutoring, computer labs, cooking classes, and debate class. To help run the program, there was a steering committee of a teacher chairperson, teachers, supervisors, paraprofessionals, guidance counselor, and principal. The grant was $350,000 for one year. And then the chancellor from NYC granted us another $100,000 the following year. The beauty of this program is the stigma of being labeled *special education* was gone. In addition, we followed a percentage of students, and they did very well in high school and did not drop out. Several educators visited the program from as far away as Germany and several educators around NYC and other states. We even had a visit from the assistant secretary of education from Washington, DC. I was awarded Principal of the Year by then mayor Giuliani for this special program.

This program was about integrating and not separating by a label, having all students and teachers working together. No one was interested in finding fault or criticizing a group of people. It makes no sense! Many of the students came from different backgrounds, but it did not matter to them. They were focused on succeeding. That's what they had in common. And they felt proud.

The second program I would like to describe was a $1,000,000 grant shared among three schools, one high school and two middle schools. It was a program to motivate students to go to college. It emphasized seventh grade the time to start to educate these students about college. The program had college students come to our school twice a week after school to tutor some students from the seventh grade. Of course, we got permission from the parents for the students to remain after school. We also had a dance class in the auditorium headed by a professional dance group.

We had a computer class sponsored by NYU to teach students how to create programs. I brought in a program sponsored by *Redbook* magazine where the class was taught by the editor in chief and the art director how to set up a magazine, which taught writing skills and several other skills. Our seventh-grade guidance counselor and bilingual counselor also worked after school under this grant to talk to students about college choices. Several students were followed through high school to chart their success and applications to colleges. Again, students in this group did very well through high school and did not drop out.

The success of this program was having students motivated through the activities of the program, such as working with college students in many of the after-school programs, along with many successful individuals! They were happy and truly wanted to succeed! No one was angry about race issues, and they did not want to be divided by race but rather by classes and interest areas.

Another program I would like to discuss is the Project Art Grant. Through this grant, a website was created called Gallery 61 to showcase some of the most amazing artwork our students have created. Each year, many of our graduating students were accepted into New York City's finest art high schools. In fact, one year, one of our students won the all-city middle school art contest. I have this permanently displayed in my apartment today. The theme was my neighborhood. It is truly an amazing art piece. Many different mediums were used. Many of our students excelled in the arts. We were even granted special art printers by our local councilwoman at that time. Students can express themselves through art. And many of the students in the middle school where I was principal were so talented and could express themselves through the arts.

I also would like to address the issue of parent involvement in education. Parents are not terrorists for caring about their children and wanting the best for them. One of the most successful schools in our country several years ago was successful because of parental involvement. I always invited parents in to discuss issues. Parents could make appointments and visit classrooms as well. Years ago, when I was teaching a special education math class, I had one student I could not control. He would bang his head on the door and would never sit down. I called his mother and invited her to visit the class and sit next to him. She asked me if she could do that every day because she would like to learn math. I said, "OK, we will try it!" She came in the next day, and her son went right to his seat and sat down next to her. All of the students were exceptionally quiet, totally focused on the lesson. They were shocked that a mother wanted to stay in the classroom with her son but liked that she was there! I had the most beautiful classroom for the rest of the term!

In another classroom, I had a female student who was very nasty and uncooperative. I actually removed her from the classroom. I called the parent that night about her behavior. The parent came in the next day and sat in the classroom and then asked me to call her every night to check up on her behavior. Students are proud to have their parents involved. It shows that they care. The student went on to graduate and dress up and got a job for twelve dollars an hour in hospitality at Trump Tower in Manhattan. That took place around 1987.

Our students did not need to have added to the curriculum critical race theory or woke. They spoke through art classes and special programs and some great classroom teachers and did not focus on negativity!

Every student has some innate talent or ability or sense of wanting to be successful! I learned that when I taught a special education math class in high school. There was one day a week that the class was broken up into three or four groups. It was called Math Contest Day. It was based on the week's homework and classwork. I assigned one leader to each group, and only that individual could call out the answer for the group. The flash card was displayed by me, and they had five minutes to answer. If someone else called out, points were deducted for them. Whatever group received the most certificates of winning on the bulletin board received a small prize. And at the end of the term, whoever had the most winning certificates received another prize. One of my toughest students who everyone thought did not care threw a chair over because his group lost and he wanted to win! That taught me a lesson. Students want to succeed, and that does not depend on race or anger toward another group of people or race.

Our country has been turning the corner on the racial issue. Yes, it is not completely there yet. But to me, adding critical race theory to the curriculum is a giant step backward and makes no sense. It will take away from the building blocks students need to learn reading, math, writing skills, and other areas of education to be successful. Our country can't be brought down by the economy, so the socialists and left wing must find a more sensitive area to separate and divide our country—racial issues! Do not let the concept of woke turn into anger! Do not turn it into prejudice toward other people and become racist in reverse. We must go in the direction of Martin Luther King, black and white walking hand in hand.

Beware that many of you are being used and brainwashed to help divide this country. Karl Marx would be proud!

Democrats versus Republicans

When I was a thirteen-year-old teenager, John F. Kennedy ran for the office of president of the United States. He was a bright, young candidate who promised a great hope for the US. He promised us a Camelot—a society in perfect harmony (utopia).

I remember my family was so excited about him running for president! A storybook president. My father took my sister and me to New Castle County Airport in Wilmington, Delaware, in 1960 to see then candidate John F. Kennedy. We were all so very excited. What a fantastic speaker! Actually, he appeared like a celebrity—someone famous. We were in awe of him. Today he would be considered a conservative Republican. That's how far left the Democratic Party has gone, especially with our present-day president, Joe Biden, and our present-day Congress.

"Ask not what your country can do for you. Ask what you can do for your country!" This John F. Kennedy quote is reversed today. Many of our citizens today feel they are entitled to money and things without working for them. In addition to this is the influx of millions of illegal immigrants, many of whom will be desperate for money and housing. They will all take, take, take! And our present-day government wants to give, give, give ... and control! The perfect storm for the uprising of socialism and communism! Beware!

Let me be perfectly clear: our democracy is in peril. Sinister forces are facing us, the American people, everywhere in the government. The Federal Bureau of Investigation and Department of Justice are corrupt. Many members of Congress are creatures of the swamp Donald Trump pledged to drain. The left-wing politicians pose as Democrats but are actually socialists and communists. They are now joined by RINO Republicans (Republican in name only) helping to pass bills such as the Infrastructure Bill, because the Democratic squad refused to vote for this bill. Thirteen Republicans (RINOs) passed the bill. The House succeeded in impeaching Donald Trump, but the Senate acquitted him.

From his first day in office, they strove to destroy this honorable man. The phony Russian collusion charges and the fake Steele dossier were attempts to discredit him as a man unfit for the presidency, and now it has been confirmed by the FBI and DOJ. In short, these villains were hell-bent on destroying him since the 2016 election. Moreover, the Democrats throughout the country hated him for his successful policies. Big Tech (Facebook, Twitter, et al.) poured millions of dollars into the Democrat coffers because they feared the true Republicans would break up their monopolies of social media. Left-wing TV programs and newspapers attacked Trump every day in every way.

In the meantime, socialist and liberal professors poisoned the minds of their students with their propaganda. Conservative professors were driven out of colleges by brainwashed students. The administrators of these colleges were not liberal but left-wing senators. Today they are beginning to prove there was fraud, and the states are waking up!

The 2020 presidential race and seats in the Senate were fraught with massive voter fraud committed in Democratic cities and states, resulting in Biden's victory and Georgia electing two left-wing senators.

Chuck Schumer, a Democratic senator from New York, boasted, "Democrats would take the Senate and change America." What he meant was that socialists and communists would seize power. The two socialists elected in Georgia tipped the scales in their favor. One of them claims to be a minister. How could a Christian minister invite the atheist communist, Fidel Castro, to speak to his congregation in his church? This minister was quoted as saying a man in the military cannot serve God. He misquoted the Bible verse that states that a person cannot serve God and mammon (money). Millions of registered Democrats in America, wake up!

Biden has opened borders and has kept them open in spite of the Supreme Court vote to keep Remain in Mexico (Trump's program). Biden just ignores this. He wants to grant illegal people amnesty to become legal citizens. He wants to make Washington, DC, and Puerto Rico states to assure four more Democrats in the Senate. He wants to repeal the deregulation of companies and federal agencies Trump enacted. He wants to cripple the Republican Party. Furthermore, he wants to fund the $1.7 trillion Green New Deal by taxing the middle class—you and me. The super-rich billionaires and giant corporations have tax loopholes to evade paying taxes. The poor don't have money to pay taxes. Instead, they need government assistance to survive.

As for trade with China, Biden will go soft with China since he and his family have business ties with the Chinese. Hence, no more sanctions on China despite the Chinese Communist Party suppressing the freedom of the Chinese people. China has concentration camps for perceived dissidents. The Muslims, Uyghur people, the people of Tibet, and now Hong Kong residents are subject to arrest, torture, and death!

All Americans should know that socialism means a tyrannical government will rule the people. The government will control the means of production by controlling the major corporations.

Owners of small businesses will end up bankrupt, even though the government will initially give stimulus money to them and the unemployed. The Federal Reserve will continue to print money and purchase treasury bonds to bloat the money supply. Our national debt is exploding—$30 trillion and counting. Our future generations will be born with hundreds of thousands of debt straddling them. Inflation will skyrocket as the value of the dollar plummets. All of these horrible things are soon to happen. Four more years of Democratic control of the presidential executive orders and Congress spell disaster for the US economy. Democrats, beware! You are destroying the future of your grandchildren. A wealth tax looms, and higher taxes for the middle class, Democrats and Republicans, are in the offing. Beware!

Everyone should read *Countdown to Socialism* by Devin Nunes and *The Case Against Socialism* by Rand Paul. They are both Republican congressmen. After reading these books, I am convinced that the so-called Democratic Party is actually a new socialist party comprised of left-wing progressives, socialists, and communists. The Democrats of the era of FDR are long gone. The majority of Americans are still rugged individualists who uphold the US Constitution and believe in God. We detest media tycoons and their celebrity sycophants. We will not be slaves of totalitarian governments, as are the people of China, Cuba, and Venezuela. The Democrats have stolen the elections of 2020, but they will not steal the souls of the American people, especially the military, the national police forces, and the Second Amendment Americans who bear arms for self-defense. Socialists and communists, beware! As for President Trump inciting a riot, he told his audience to go to the Capitol in a peaceful protest. Yes!

Unfortunately, left-wing thugs wearing MAGA hats infiltrated the marches and broke into the Capitol, destroying property and killing people. One of them, John Sullivan, was an Antifa activist. This lunatic actually bragged about posing as a Trump supporter while videotaping himself. Sullivan, who uses the name "Jayden

X" on the app, can be heard cursing and inciting violence in the US Capitol. Of course, Antifa and Black Lives Matter deny any complicity. The mainstream media refuses to report these facts. The FBI continues to ignore these facts too. What a pity that the Republicans had no opportunity to present solid evidence of voting fraud because of the riots and had to flee for their lives.

When Antifa and Black Lives Matter protestors burned and looted small businesses and attacked and injured many police officers in Democratic-controlled cities like New York City, Los Angeles, Portland, and Seattle, Democratic congressmen, governors, and majors were mute the entire time. Of course, the left-wing media described the protestors as mostly peaceful. When the Speaker of the House, Nancy Pelosi, was questioned by reporters about vandals toppling statues they hated, like Christopher Columbus in Baltimore, where she comes from, Pelosi retorted, "People do what they do." Senator Schumer took the cake when he angrily screamed at reporters, "First we take the Senate, then we change America." Change America? Yes, from a democracy to a tyranny of socialism. He is a socialist posing as a Democrat.

At least Bernie Sanders does not conceal the truth. He is a socialist Democrat who had his honeymoon in Moscow! All I can repeat is that democracy is in grave peril.

I must emphasize that Donald Trump did not urge his supporters to storm the Capitol on January 6, 2021. Yes, he encouraged them to march to the Capitol peacefully and stay outside the building peacefully. And, again, I believe this was instigated by John Sullivan / Antifa.

The last thing he wanted for them was to disrupt the congressional investigation by the Republicans who would offer evidence of this disgraceful fraud committed by Democrat operatives. The Democrats and RINOs have used these fake claims to impeach Trump for a second time to defame him and his legacy as president of the United States. Trump has exhorted his supporters *never* to engage in violence, especially last year when the leftists rioted multiple times in Washington, DC. Republican supporters of Trump have never burned down buildings and looted small businesses in any city in The United States. The media will never mention this inconvenient truth. Trump has always stressed law and order at his peaceful mass rallies.

These peaceful events have often been worked by leftists in counterprotests. The mass media (fake news) has never reported this sad news because they support the Democrats. Period. Remember, John Earle Sullivan, founder of Insurgence USA, was present at the Capitol, wearing a MAGA hat and screaming, "We gotta get this shit burned!" and "We got to rid that motherfucker out of office!" He has been arrested, and there are sworn affidavits of these facts. Of course, the mass media will never reveal these facts. John Earle Sullivan has been charged with entering a restricted building, civil discords, and violent disorderly conduct.

I want my readers to know that we subscribed to the *New York Times* for many years. However, when the *New York Times* would not inform its readers about Hunter Biden and his family's connection with the Chinese Communist Party (CCP) and sordid scandals, we canceled our subscription.

Now we read the *New York Post* and *Epoch Times* because the print the unvarnished truth with zero coverups. If you voted for the Left, here's what you voted for in Biden's executive order: 1) Ready to vote to deploy troops to the Middle East. In other words, engage in another war. 2) Biden rejoined the World Health Organization, which failed to warn the United States about the pandemic. 3) Biden rejoined the Paris Climate Accords, with the United States paying the highest fees. 4) Biden rejoined the Trans-Pacific Partnership (TPP), which would result in our massive job loss to China (here we go again). 5) Biden's executive order allows men with wigs to enter girls' restrooms and compete in women's sports. 6) Biden wants to charge a hefty fine for not having health insurance (the previous penalty under Obamacare).

Biden has revoked the Keystone Pipeline, resulting in the loss of eleven thousand jobs. The oil will be transported by railroads and trucks, which is more dangerous and expensive. Biden has increased corporate taxes, income taxes and payroll taxes, and small business taxes dramatically.

Small businesses will severely lay off workers and/or pass off this increase to the consumer, and capital gains and dividend taxes have increased greatly. This will discourage people from investing in stocks and bonds, resulting in the markets declining 10 percent (correction) or 20 percent (recession) and possibly a depression! There is no question that, regardless of what anyone may think of his presidency, Donald Trump's foreign policy accomplishments were exemplary and second to none in the modern era. In addition to keeping America out of new wars, he managed to reduce our military footprint in places we should have pulled out of more than a decade ago.

Trump negotiated peace treaties between the Jews and Arabs. Four nations are now living in peace and harmony. All will improve their economies with trade deals and commerce. Do not expect Joe Biden to negotiate any more peace treaties with the Jews and Arabs. He will send more American troops to fight and die in the Middle East. He is under pressure from the left-wing Muslim Democratic congressmen to side with Palestine. If Donald Trump were our president, there would be additional Arab states at peace with Israel. Well, at least for the time being, the United Arab Emirates, Bahrain, Sudan, and Israel have achieved peace. Only Donald Trump can make peace with all the Arab nations and Israel in the Middle East. I pray this will come to fruition when Donald Trump is reelected president of the United States in 2024.

Last spring, as the Supreme Court was preparing to hear oral arguments in a monumental case that would have significantly impact abortion rights in the United States, Schumer, a Democrat senator from New York, spoke out against Associated Justice Neil Gorsuch and Bret Kavanaugh using inflammatory language. "I want to tell you, Gorsuch and Kavanaugh, you have released the whirlwind and will pay the price," Schumer said at a proabortion rally. "You won't know what hit you if you go forward with these awful decisions."

In a rare response, Chief Justice Roberts spoke out against Schumer for "dangerous rhetoric." Justices know that criticism comes with the territory, but threatening statements of this sort from the highest levels of government are not only inappropriate but also dangerous. All members of the court will continue to do their job, without fear or favor from whatever quarter. Speaking on *Fox News Sunday*, Rand Paul said if Democrats' impeachment standard was fair, Schumer should also be impeached and put on trial for incitement to riot since a violent mob tried to invade the Supreme Court after Schumer spoke in front of the Supreme Court. Rand Paul said that Democrats would not hold Schumer or other Democrat lawmakers accountable for their inflammatory rhetoric, citing Representatives Ilhan Omar (D-Minnesota) and Maxine Waters (D-California).

There are major differences between the Democrats and Republicans historically. The Democrats were considered the party of the blue-collar working class. The Republicans were considered to be representatives of wealthy entrepreneurs and corporations. The Republicans defied powerful labor unions that worked hard to gain higher salaries and fringe benefits, such as paid leave, health benefits, and bargaining power to an excessive degree.

Today, the lines have blurred. Many workers started their own small businesses, which often became hugely successful. They switched party allegiance. These people who were traditionally employees became employers. They were empowered by their wealth and ability to hire and fire their workers. Instead of remaining Democrats, they became Republicans. The main concern of these new wealthy owners was profitability. In the past, they would pay low wages and did not provide workers with safe working conditions or job security. This is no longer the case.

As more employees joined unions, the unions became stronger and could bargain collectively with the businessmen. The union men could go on strike and cut off the profits of the businessmen; thus, over the years, they became powerful, big forces to be reckoned with by politicians. Democrats outnumbered Republicans. There are always many more workers than employers. The unions such as the AFL-CIO and teachers' unions made major strides because they collected higher dues from their members. Shielded workers made much more money than unshielded workers. The Democrats flourished in the mid-1900s.

On the other hand, the affluent Republicans influenced the government through special-interest lobbyists. College progressors and technology workers made the highest salaries. Today, many people who are Democrats become socialists and communists. They are college educated and empowered.

By sheer numbers, they are powerful and can intimidate politicians who oppose them. Today, the Democrats have elected more presidents and congressmen than the Republicans. Time is on their side, as the migration laws have become lax. Donald Trump enforced legal immigration, while Joe Biden grants amnesty and the power to vote to illegal immigrants. The Democrats want open borders. They have ensured the votes of legal and illegal immigrants who cross the Mexican border. These people are welcomed to the United States by Joe Biden and majority-Democrat Congress. These people want to escape poverty and violence from the drug cartels.

Who can blame them? The number of immigrants who cross the border into the United States dropped under Donald Trump and has dramatically increased under Joe Biden. These people join caravans to cross the Mexico/US border by catch-and-release policy in the border patrol police.

Many of the illegal immigrants don't show up for their hearings scheduled five years after they cross. They find sanctuary in California and cities across the country run by Democratic governors and majors. If Texas turns blue, it will join blue California and New York. These three states afford well over a hundred voters in the electoral college. If the Democrats succeed in making the District of Columbia (DC) and Puerto Rico states, there will never be another Republican president and/or Republican Congress.

Deliberately, China exports many cheap, synthetic drugs to the drug cartels in Mexico, especially fentanyl, which is forty times more powerful than crack-cocaine or heroin. Numerous Americans die every year from overdoses. The Democrats are well aware of all these facts.

The Democrats falsely claim to be the party of unity. They deny that Big Tech and mass media are on their side. They are happy that Facebook, Twitter, YouTube, Instagram, and Snapchat are on their side, censoring conservative Republicans.

If Americans read the platform of the Democrats, they will realize the sad truth. The Democrats are veering to the left. We'll become a socialist country, taxing the middle class to make the rich richer and the poor more dependent on government assistance. In his first day as president, Joe Biden fired 10,500 people who had been working on the border wall and 12,000 people who had been building the XL Keystone Pipeline, including secondary support jobs. Biden put around fifty thousand people out of work on his first day. Thus far, he has destroyed seventy thousand jobs. He refunded abortions and allowed men in girls' locker rooms. He overturned Trump's executive order that lowered the cost of insulin for diabetics.

Comparison of Current and Former Presidents

Joe Biden stopped construction of the Keystone Pipeline and border wall on our southern border with Mexico on his first day in office. This resulted in the loss of one hundred thousand jobs immediately. Biden suggests that workers can secure jobs in his proposed Green New Deal working on wind turbines and solar power panels. Biden seeks abortion on demand, including the last trimester. He wants gun rights to be subject to severe restriction. Biden has opened our southern border to illegal aliens who have not been processed. Millions of these people have spread out in the country this year alone. Some of them smuggle drugs and are involved in human trafficking. Some have already been deported from the United States. Biden wants higher taxes on people with $400,000 in income and higher corporate and capital gains taxes. He is against term limits for politicians. He is a left-wing Democrat seeking to advance the federal government and the loss of states' rights, possibly leading to socialism and communism.

Donald Trump accomplished a booming economy and low unemployment and made the US energy independent. He was tough in trade talks with communist China and stopped the flow of manufacturing jobs overseas. He is for small businesses, voter ID, and small government with less control / fewer mandates. He favors term limits for politicians and is not liberal but conservative. He sees the Green New Deal costing $50 trillion in the next ten years as the source of climbing interest rates, surging inflation, and plummeting dollar values. He wants to save our oil, natural gas, and clean coal industries and put these people back to work again. The American people are sick watching our country being destroyed.

The antithetical political positions of these two men are startling. I cannot fathom that any American citizen, Democrat or Republican, can agree with the issues and policies of President Biden. His executive orders spell disaster for our economy and democracy. I am certain that people who voted for him regret it. I can only pray that the Republicans secure the House and Senate in 2022. It's called damage control. Biden has already issued more executive orders than Trump, Obama, and Bush combined, without the consent of Congress. We have purportedly elected a president, not a tyrant, but that is not the case!

Speaker of the House Nancy Pelosi manifested utmost contempt for President Donald Trump while he was addressing Congress in a State of the Union speech. She tore up her copy of his speech on live television in front of seventy-five million Americans who voted for him. How disrespectful to the American people. Disgrace is an understatement!

President Trump did not stop working for us when he was hospitalized and treated for COVID-19. He was provided a room in the hospital where he could take care of government business. Thank God he recovered rapidly from this dreadful virus and was released the next day.

Summary Fact Sheet

Under Trump, the US became energy independent, producing more oil than needed—thirteen million barrels each day. We actually could export oil for the first time. Under Biden, we are energy dependent, importing oil from Saudi Arabia and Russia. Biden closed down the XL Pipeline his first day in office. He is opposed to using our vast reserves of coal, oil, and national gas. Instead, he wants to implement the Green New Deal, using wind turbines and solar panels. More than seventy thousand people in the fossil fuel industry have already lost their jobs.

Under Trump, we dropped out of the Paris Climate Treaty, which seeks to reduce car emissions. The expenses were paid mostly by the US for the transition to renewables, even though we emit only 15 percent of the world's total greenhouse gases. China, India, and other nations contribute 85 percent of carbon emissions yet are exempt from reducing carbon emissions for ten years and continue to use coal-fired plants to generate electricity.

We now have an open border with Mexico. Illegal aliens are pouring into the US unabated from countries around the world. Two million of them entered in 2021. There are thirty million illegal aliens already here. Joe Biden was ordered by the US Supreme Court to keep these people in Mexico until they are processed legally. No compliance from Joe Biden. Thousands enter every day and night without being tested for COVID. Once in this country, American taxpayers are paying to feed them, house them, and take care of their medical expenses. If they are apprehended by the border patrol, they must be released. Even criminals may not be deported.

Under Biden, inflation is soaring and supply chains are broken. Citizens will pay higher taxes, as will corporations. Our military was withdrawn from Afghanistan, leaving American citizens in Afghanistan behind. Foreign nationalist terrorists are more powerful than ever; they pose a serious threat to our national security. It is no wonder that Biden's approval rating by Americans has plummeted to 38 percent.

So you, the reader, come to your own conclusion and ask, "What is this all about?" Don't you want your country back? Or would you prefer socialism/communism to take over? And ask why these originally moderate Democrats would lean left toward socialism. I ask again, why?

Relevant Articles from AMAC magazine

"President Donald J. Trump AMAC's 2020 Man of the Year," February 2021 (volume 14, issue 1), pages 44–50, Andrew Mangione and Rebecca Weber.

"Trump's Historical Accomplishments," February 2021 (volume 15, issue 1), pages 32–34, Robert B. Charles.

"Biden's Catastrophe—No End in Sight," June 2021 (volume 15, issue 3), pages 42–46, Robert B. Charles.

"Racism and Political History," October 2021 (volume 15, issue 5), pages 12–13, Robert B. Charles.

"Alert: Interest on the National Debt, A Monster That is Eating Our Future," October 2021 (volume 15, issue 5), pages 16–18, Bob Carlstrom.

"Biden Pushing America from Energy Independence to Dependence," October 2021 (volume 15, issue 5), pages 22–24, Shane Harris.

"National Security America Endangered," October 2021 (volume 15, issue 5), pages 42–46, Shane Harris.

"Democrats Turn Their Backs on Cuban's Cries for Freedom," October 2021 (volume 15, issue 5), pages 48–52, Pat Manning.

"Top Five Most Harmful Biden Economic Policies," August 2021 (volume 15, issue 4), pages 12–14, Palmer Schoening.

"Racist? America is Anti-Racist," August 2021 (volume 15, issue 4), pages 18–20, Robert B. Charles.

"Critical Race Theory Seven Hard Truths," August 2021 (volume 15, issue 4), pages 42–44, Robert B. Charles.

"Seven Patterns Now Shaping the 2022 Midterms," August 2021 (volume 15, issue 4), pages 46–50, Seamus Brannan.

"The 1619 Project," August 2021 (volume 15, issue 4), pages 60–62, Jeff Szymanski.

President Donald J. Trump AMAC's 2020 Man of the Year

Harry S. Truman imparted great wisdom when he said, "Men make history and not the other way around. In periods where there is no leadership, society stands still. Progress occurs when courageous, skillful leaders seize the opportunity to change things for the better." On behalf of his great accomplishments of four years in office, President Donald J. Trump has been selected by AMAC members as AMAC's "Man of the Year." Not only has Trump succeeded in making America great again by bringing back jobs and restoring the economy, but he also secured peace in the Middle East and guided America through an unprecedented pandemic and turbulent times. Despite being challenged by the media and the left who sought to destroy his reputation, the President did not waver. Instead, he stood his ground, and in the face of many storms, proceeded to move forward to uphold principles of goodwill and justice.

When a child is born, it is every parent's dream for their offspring to grow in wisdom, courage, faith, and strength and go out into the world to achieve great things. This feeling was no different for Mary Anne and Fred Trump, who gave birth to their second-born son, Donald John Trump, on June 14, 1946. In birth order, Donald was the fourth of five children. Little did Mary Anne and Fred know that their newborn son would grow to become one of the most successful businessmen in America and the forty-fifth President of the United States. Today, Donald J. Trump embodies the caring spirit to put the people of the nation first. He has worked hard on behalf of American citizens to deliver historic results in Washington, for the nation, and for the world.

Reflecting upon Donald J. Trump's childhood, we see that Trump learned early on to be productive. Mary Anne and Fred enrolled their son in the New York Military Academy at the age of 13 to promote the family's values of hard work and discipline. Trump later began college at Fordham University and soon transferred to the University of Pennsylvania's Wharton School for its real estate studies program. Trump's success began early; as a student, he invested in Philadelphia real estate before graduating in 1968 with a bachelor's degree in economics. Trump understood that working diligently would produce positive results.

Mary Anne and Fred Trump wouldn't live to see their son, at the age of 70 and without ever having held public office, go on to win over 14,000,000 votes in the 2016 Republican presidential primaries, the most votes received for any Republican primary candidate. Today, at the age of 74, Donald is the proud father of 5 children and grandfather to 10, and he holds the title "President of the United States of America." Throughout his life, he continually sets the bar high and embraces the self-ascribed philosophy that, "As long as you are going to be thinking anyway, think big."

But it is not because of Donald Trump's status or fame that AMAC members overwhelmingly chose the forty-fifth President as their Man of the Year for 2020. Rather, it is because AMAC members put their hope and trust in him—and he delivered. In an AMAC Weekly Newsletter poll sent via email on November 24, 2020, and posted on the www.amac.us website, President Trump received 34,123 of the 42,187 votes cast, easily outpacing second-place finisher "Essential Workers."

It is not difficult to understand the esteem AMAC members have for President Trump, given all he has done for mature Americans during his time in office. His accomplishments can be listed, many of which were well documented in these pages, but Donald Trump's achievements are only part of what makes him one of the greatest men to have ever lived. Rather, it is his unique abilities and character traits that have allowed him to accomplish more than anyone could have imagined.

In our lifetimes, we would be hard pressed to witness another leader as effective as Trump. Leadership takes vision, and Trump's is 20/20. He saw the potential for how America could exist, and then took steps to get us there, which required discipline and decisiveness. He saw things that no one else saw, and he recognized that he needed to align others with his vision. It has been said that great visionaries will always meet opposition from weak minds, but the seeds they plant can save the world.

While critics will play down Trump's leadership style, one thing that cannot be ignored is the fact that he can and does lead. No other US President has ever received as many undisputed votes as Donald J. Trump—a testament to his resiliency, confidence, and unwavering commitment to the promise he made to the American people: to make America stronger, prouder, and greater than ever before.

Donald J. Trump understood that the American people were tired of bad leadership in our government and recognized that the government is not the solution to our problems; instead, he grasped that government was the problem. He helped to shape a public opinion that united Americans who were tired of government invading their lives and not representing their ideas and values.

Defeating 16 primary candidates for President of the United States, Trump has been much more than talk and more about action, a quality that earned him the trust of the majority of the American people. He took a leadership role to serve the best interests of Americans, and he delivered with thought, hard decision making, and courage.

Trumpism is a new term for the political ideology, style of governance, political movement, and set of mechanisms for acquiring and keeping power that are associated with Donald Trump. It is a bold and profoundly different way of thinking. His common sense blended with the determination to win, along with a brave heart and unforgiving honesty, propelled him to take action in the face of horrible opposition because of his unyielding promise to all Americans to make America great. He is a unique American leader. No one has ever won the Presidency without having held public office or served as a general in the military. His leadership style alone is what drew people to him. He understood what the vast majority of Americans wanted, and after spending a lifetime of understanding how to give people what they want, did he deliver!

President Trump's notable achievements are too many to mention, but for AMAC's membership, he delivered again and again, including driving down Medicare Advantage and Part D premiums to historic lows while increasing plan choices. His policies also led to drastically lowering the cost of insulin for Medicare beneficiaries. He established the Rebate Rule through an executive order that requires pharmacy benefit managers to share the rebates they receive from drug companies with Medicare beneficiaries at the pharmacy counter to lower their out-of-pocket expenses.

Another executive order created price transparency for shoppable medical services, which allows American patients to choose the best price and physician prior to having a procedure. There are numerous other policy examples that demonstrate President Trump's commitment to caring for America's seniors.

President Trump did so much more in addition to enacting smart policies. Through his status as an outsider, he showed the world that one does not have to come up through the customary political ranks to attain the highest office in the United States. He challenged an ingrained establishment that was bent on destroying him, his family, and members of his administration by engineering a thriving pre-pandemic economy and scoring significant Middle East foreign policy victories in a relatively short period of time. He told Americans that a COVID-19 vaccine would be ready for distribution by the end of 2020. While his detractors mocked him for making such a claim, he developed Operation Warp Speed, which removed the regulatory obstacles and contributed to making his prediction become a reality.

President Trump's election was the result of a conservative populist political movement, seen by many as ordinary citizens fighting back against a powerful, elite establishment that made numerous promises but delivered nothing. Trump picked up this mantle and, in the process of delivering significant policy results, uncovered the systemic corruption of the establishment and the evil scheming of the Deep State. His actions reverberated among diverse Americans and resulted in increased support for him among Black, Hispanic, and Asian voters. A strong supporter of our Second Amendment rights, Trump was the first sitting president to attend an NRA convention since Ronald Reagan; the first US President ever to appoint a Hasidic Jew, Mitchell Silk, to a senior slot in the administration; and the first sitting President to attend the March for Life rally, stating, "Unborn children have never had a stronger defender in the White House and as the Bible tells us, each person is wonderfully made," adding, "We are here for a very simple reason: to defend the right of every child, born and unborn, to fulfill their God-given potential." Along the way to generating the most votes ever received by any incumbent president, Trump captured about 30 percent of the vote among the LGBT community. The diversity of this movement Trump expanded is important, as it exemplifies its unanimity and ensures its propagation.

Donald J. Trump displays strong common sense and applies this kind of thinking to life's challenges. He was once quoted as saying, "Watch somebody sell their used car and not wash it. You can spend $10 washing the car and get another

$200 for the car." Both in private life and in business, Trump has never been afraid to offer a piece of his mind, as witnessed in his response to NFL players for kneeling for the national anthem and team owners for not requiring that players stand: "The American public is fed up with the disrespect the NFL is paying to our country, our flag, and our national anthem. Weak and out of control!"

In acknowledgment of the credibility of Trump's "America First" approach to domestic and foreign policy, Joe Biden said, "I want to make sure we're going to fight like hell by investing in America first," in an interview regarding foreign trade after the election. Biden uttered these words after routinely attacking this strategy during the presidential campaign. The fact that Republicans did so well down ballot is further evidence of the strength of the populist movement. The predicted "blue wave" never materialized, as solidly conservative representatives, some of them women, were elected to shrink the Democrat House majority.

Most conservatives are aware of the bias toward their ideology—and Republicans in general—that exists in mainstream American journalism. It was on vicious display beginning with Trump's announcement to run for President and grew louder after he was elected. The criticism he received for his handling of the coronavirus was particularly shrill—until it wasn't. President Trump has been a vocal critic of state lockdowns and school closings, two issues for which he was roundly condemned. However, now we see mainstream journalists like Nicholas Kristof of the New York Times agreeing with Trump that schools are not significant sources of transmission for the virus. The Times also published a story questioning the logic of banning small gatherings. Even CNN's Jake Tapper gave President Trump credit for vaccine delivery after habitually criticizing the administration's efforts to fight the virus.

These are not just a few instances of members of the media agreeing with President Trump. They are much more than that. They are demonstrable proof that Trump has broken the mainstream media and destroyed their credibility. He knew early on that the media would not fairly report on any aspect of his administration, so instead of trying to manage them like other Republicans, he exposed their agenda and labeled their efforts as "fake news" through the masterful use of his Twitter account. This characterization has had a huge impact on how Americans perceive the news they receive from mainstream outlets.

The Trump presidency has had an enormous effect on the Democrat Party. Their years-long affliction with Trump Derangement Syndrome has laid bare their arsenal of strategies and tactics used to "get" Trump for the whole world to witness. Spying, lying, fake stories of "Russian collusion," contrived impeachment charges, Big Tech censorship, phony polls, and the granddaddy of them all—apparent concerted election fraud operations in battleground states—are all on display courtesy of America's Democrat Party.

Indeed, Trump's battle for election integrity exposes the Democrats' debasing clutch on another American institution, and his fight could have lasting implications for generations to come.

He broke the Democrats with his three Supreme Court nominations. Where other

Presidents may have withdrawn nominees in the face of caterwauling from Democrats serving on the Judiciary Committee, Trump remained steadfast in his support of his selected jurists. In the face of outrageous allegations and wholly inappropriate questioning, Trump was undeterred and watched as the Democrats twisted and contorted into caricatures of themselves. His commitment was rewarded when his three nominees were confirmed and are now serving lifetime appointments on the highest court in the land.

Donald J. Trump's arrival on the American political scene was a gamechanger. His standing as a businessman with a reputation for getting things done was welcomed as a breath of fresh air for his supporters and seen as a mortal threat for those wishing to continue business-as-usual in Washington. Some found the brash New Yorker's personality and accompanying social media presence arrogant and self-promoting, while others appreciated his ability to fight back against his attackers.

Perhaps it is this characteristic of not backing down from a confrontation that has so endeared President Trump to AMAC members. While he is not perfect—no President is— Trump has shown a profound love of America and inspired patriotism not experienced since the days of Ronald Reagan. Even more meaningful is that this self-made American success story did not seek the presidency to enrich himself. He left a relatively quiet, comfortable life because he felt America needed him to make the country great again.

As his many successes stand on their own merits, he has risen to serve a great purpose, and well over 70 million Americans were enlightened because of his bold and courageous leadership. For the faithful and for those who believe in divine purpose, Donald J. Trump's role as President of the United States of America is nothing short of God using him for His glory and His good. To AMACs "Man of the Year," we thank you, Mr. President! May God bless you! (*AMAC*—Andrew Mangione and Rebecca Weber)

Trump's Historical Accomplishments

Whether you love him, hate him, or fall some-where between these two extremes, Donald Trump has been one of the most objectively can-do, achievement-focused presidents in American history.

With resolution, facing a relentless partisan storm, he managed—in just four years—to remake the federal judiciary, rebuild the American econ-omy, reshape the Middle East, end the ISIS territo-rial caliphate, educate Americans on China's true aims, reorient allied defense contributions and expectations, bring American troops home, end Iran's free pass on nuclear weapons, halt runaway North Korean missile and nuclear tests, secure the southern border, and affirm fundamentals in our Bill of Rights, including free speech, free exer-cise of religion, freedom of assembly, the Second Amendment, and transparency in criminal justice.

To that, add a politically incorrect—that is, freedom-centric--approach to public dialogue, often blunt, impolite, and unpolished but authen-tic in an age of plastic talk. Trump elevated the public's understanding of media bias, dishonesty, and partisanship. He defended unborn children, articulated why America's founding generation was unrivaled, and paid tribute to America's vet-erans and law enforcement communities, as well as the nation's exceptional, entrepreneurial, and risk-taking spirit. He apologized to no one for America's greatness.

Concretely, President Trump secured the pas-sage of the largest tax relief bill since Ronald Reagan, unremittingly rolled back federal regulations, and triggered the fastest, broadest economic recovery on record, boosting employment across virtually every sector and demographic, along with increasing business creation, personal income, and stocks and returning US capital invested abroad.

His initiative cut corporate tax rates to 21 percent from 35 percent, creating powerful incentives to hire, invest, rehire, and reinvest. Against the odds, labor productivity rose; which liberal economists had said was "impossible," while inflation remained in check and growth exploded.

Dozens of data points prove the "middle-class miracle" that was Trump's economy. Topping the list is wage growth. Liberals swore Trump could not raise wages—yet he did. Inflation-adjusted wage growth since 1980 averaged $4.05 per quarter. Under Obama, it was $3.20 per quarter. In Trump's first three years, wage growth averaged a staggering $690 per quarter.

Even when brought low by coronavirus, Trump's economy kept employers and stocks afloat. Month by month, Americans have clawed back, with faith in economic fundamentals and prayers that state lockdowns will end. While Trump was blamed for not federalizing the COVID-19 response, he honored the 10th Amendment, which bars federal mandates where power is constitutionally reserved to the states and people.

One layer deeper, Americans will have this president to thank for significant new understandings. No longer will Americans assume their federal government, without oversight, is on the right track. Trump made clear–and ironically, his impeachment affirmed—that due process, openness, and honesty in government are not always present. They should be.

Trump began restoring our federal judiciary to its non-activist, constitutionally limited origins, nominating and confirming 220 federal judges and filling 25 percent of the federal bench, including nominating 53 judges to the 12 federal circuits, as well as adding three Supreme Court Justices.

For perspective, while presidents have done more over two terms, few have done as much in one. A breakdown shows that FDR appointed eight justices in four terms, Eisenhower, Taft, and Grant appointed five in two, and others appointed three or four in two, but Obama, both Bushes, Clinton, Johnson, and Kennedy only got two justices, and others got one. Trump has influenced the future mightily with judges.

Similarly, Trump's speeches, such as in Saudi Arabia and Poland, have been epic. Years from now, when historians cull his presidential papers, these speeches will stand out, as will his States of the Union, all historically grounded, idealistic, optimistic, and other-regarding in tone. Trump reminded us to remember, to revere, and to celebrate America's past, taking lessons from it.

On the international stage, many, decry Trump's protective trade policies, willingness to speak of American exceptionalism, power comparisons, 'national self-interest, and closing endless wars. The truth is, he has made valid points.

Even if the world is interconnected, laws of comparative advantage—in sectors like energy production, manufacturing, and services still matter, as does rule of law, generally. Truth matters. If something is wrong, and the international community is party to that wrongness, it needs calling out. In places like the UN, WTO, and WHO, Trump did that.

With respect to ensuring US national security and buttressing collective security among allies, Trump was impolitely frank, often unnecessarily public, but his points were neither inapt nor arcane. Alliances only work when allies keep their word, and he sought that assurance from NATO and in numerous bilateral contexts. He put teeth behind UN and unilateral sanctions.

Other firsts include creating the Space Force, the first new military branch since 1947; architecting a new moon landing, planned for one man and one woman; killing two of the world's most infamous terrorist leaders, Abu Bakr al-Baghdadi and Qasem Soleimani; and assisting countless patriotic state legislators, governors, mayors, and members of Congress to win elections on the basic credo of maintaining America's greatness.

In this process, Trump realigned the Republican Party, bringing into the fold more former Democrats and Independents; Black; Hispanic, Asian, and other minority voters; union members; law enforcement officers; veterans; young idealists; and older patriots, all bound together by their love of, appreciation for, and hope in our constitutional freedoms, opportunity, and individual liberty.

In a word, being something other than an ordinary, traditional politician, taking risks no president has taken in decades, speaking candidly, questioning assumptions, and pushing new ideas in economics, foreign policy, national and border security, public dialogue, and government transparency, Trump brought hope to many who had lost it. The mission now is to hold that hope. In the end, that is what idealists, patriots, and citizens do–they, look backward with gratitude and forward with hope. (*AMAC*–Robert B. Charles)

Biden's Catastrophe—No End in Sight

Realism is a better guide to policy than anger, resentment, hope, or misplaced compassion. The problem of illegal immigration is not new, but the rate of inflow—the sudden surge in illegal migration over the southern border—is. Two questions nag: What is the cost, and how do we stop it? Let us talk costs first, as numbers offer room for agreement. The immediate and projected costs are measurable and can be reasonably estimated. Some are tangible—the impact on health care, education, crime, drug trafficking, state taxes, and community cohesion. Some are intangible - reduced respect for law, citizenship, naturalization, and elevated risk of election manipulation and fraud.

Historically, modern America has experienced shifting levels of legal and illegal immigration. Legal immigrants tend to be law-abiding, patriotic, quick to assimilate, and dedicated to learning English, American history, and civic requirements, as well as working, paying taxes, serving in the military, and avoiding dependence on the state. Illegal immigrants, by the numbers, tend toward shadows, often following a path from illegal entry to dependence, seeking refuge in "sanctuary cities," and being less quick to assimilate, speak English, know American history, contribute civically, pay taxes, or serve in the military.

Overall, tangible estimates indicate an illegal alien population of 14.5 million, imposing a measurable cost of $133 billion on citizen taxpayers.

The Federation for American Immigration Reform has tracked rising costs over a decade, separating them into discrete categories. For example, they estimated the 2016 cost of educating the children of illegal immigrants in public schools at $59.8 billion, with 98.9 percent of that cost met by state and local taxes.

Unaccompanied minors, especially from Guatemala, Honduras, and El Salvador—crossing from Mexico—have weighed down formerly healthy educational systems, requiring intensive resource draws to teach English, maintain discipline, and address unique health and development issues. Notably, costs above are for 2016, which saw 118,929 unaccompanied minors.

Parallel numbers are offered by think tanks like the American Enterprise Institute, which pegged illegal immigrant health costs at nearly $20 billion when local, state, and federal benefits are tallied, with federal benefits tapped through clever state-level cost-shifting. All numbers are higher for 2021.

The secondary tangible costs include, for example, the elevated social and tax burdens associated with detention, sanctuary cities, increased homelessness, and affiliation with drug trafficking and gang crime, as well as elevated police training, deployment, adjudication, deportation, and social services. The intangible costs are equally daunting. How does one measure reduced respect for law and the ripple of crimes committed without punishment, or any material consequence, on future crime? What about the influence of unassimilated populations, and groups encouraged not to assimilate, on a wider community? Or the effect on the contiguous communities of sanctuary cities, where health, safety, crime, homelessness, social unrest, unemployment, and falling property values overflow? In short, how do you measure all the intangibles?

Taken as a whole, the basic understanding must be that illegal immigration, as opposed to legal immigration, undermines fundamental premises on which civic order, public health and safety, citizenship, lawful behavior, and a secure, prosperous, law-abiding population depend. Illegal immigration also presents material concerns for the electoral process, since election cycles regularly record illegal alien voting. As margins tighten, small changes have larger effects.

The immediate concern is that, knowing all this, the Biden Administration is actively encouraging an unprecedented surge in illegal migration over the southwestern border. Perspective is important. On one hand, we are nation of roughly 330 million citizens encountering an illegal inflow of over 100,000 per month. On the other hand, the inflow is rising, while deterrence, assimilation, strategic planning, health, policing, housing, and the quality of affected educational systems are all falling.

The overall numbers, and the costs they impose on society, are unequivocally rising. Moreover, risks to citizens and illegal aliens are rising in tandem, as both populations face crime, health, integration, and assimilation challenges. We cannot look away. This is a crisis.

The policies creating this crisis are clear. Biden's suspension of the Trump agreement with Mexico to hold applicants pending asylum, resurrecting the so-called "catch and release" policy, is resulting in mass illegal resettlement. That was the first misstep. The second was promising to absorb unaccompanied minors, pushing them to the heartland through churches, civic groups, attenuated relatives, and sometimes bus drops. That policy's effect, intended or not, has been to encourage an explosion at the border. Human traffickers are working overtime.

The current numbers are sobering, to the point of demanding a response, a responsible reaction, or the cone of illegal migration will keep widening.

The world is awash in billions of impoverished humans, all of whom would love to know that our southern border is wide open.

Again, the numbers put the crisis in perspective. US Customs and Border Patrol encountered 172,000 migrants in March 2021, a 71 percent jump over February, itself seeing over 100,000 illegal crossings. Late spring saw the highest numbers in 15 years—March saw almost 20,000 minors.

Month on month, unaccompanied minors overwhelm housing and continue to be bussed across America—many with COVID-19 and most with no records, parents, or means. These aren't just lost asylum seekers, either, as 98 percent show up between ports of entry, many injured or worse. So, who is responsible for this mass tragedy, illegal invitation, and damaging impact on American civic order, health, safety, education, assimilation, devaluing legal immigration, naturalization, and rule of law? Who must stop this policy error, human tragedy, and failed messaging to the world? Whom should Americans hold responsible? Is there any question?

To be clear, this is not a local or state policy, nor the work of a governor, state legislature, or inattentive law enforcement. This failure is entirely the work of the Biden White House and the complicit Senate and House Democrats. They have pushed this abomination, an anti-legal approach to immigration, on the American people. They know it, they avert it, and most will not talk about it—neither the president nor the vice president will spend material time at the border and we, the American people, are told to pipe down, pony up, and deal with it. The bottom line is that solutions exist to this crisis, and we can help push them.

Congressional representatives and senators are accountable to us, and we can make clear that this policy undermines citizenship, civic order, public health, safety, and respect for law. State legislatures and governors can be forced to challenge federal decisions, deploy state resources, support federal law enforcement, and message a "stop" signal, not "keep coming."

Finally, a deep breath is worth taking. The numbers prove a disproportionate upward spike in the illegal human inflow, with tangible and intangible costs being felt across America. They also support the inference of rising intangible costs. But we can stop this and reverse the policy. We know who bears responsibility for this human train wreck.

Stepping up, speaking up, writing, and registering what we know is the best way to get to common sense, helping fellow citizens and—in ways no one will even acknowledge—helping those victimized in transit. If we believe in law and the moral and civic underpinnings of our legal system, we need to tell those pushing illegality to stop—especially when they are at the top. Realism is a better guide to policy than misplaced compassion. The time is now for accountability. (*AMAC*—Robert B. Charles)

Racism and Political History

When caught in sea fog, one turns to the compass. When caught in political fog, one turns to history. On racism, historical facts should be our compass—they describe where we have been, where we are, and point to where we should be, as well as how we get there. Racism is wrong and has always been wrong, since it replaces assurances of equality, respect, dignity, and honor with prejudice, persecution, pernicious actions, and an assumption that inequality—even implicit inequality— is permissible. In America, inequality is never permissible. That is why so many strive so valiantly— in personal and professional lives—to fulfill the constitutional promise of "equal treatment" under the law, America's most solemn promise. History puts a spotlight—or should— on those who have blocked "equal protection" under the law, in the words of our 5th and 14th Amendments. Modern media seem intent on rewriting history, casting Republicans as racist, but that is not what history shows. History is painfully clear. A refresher seems timely. In the late 19th and early 20th centuries, the Democratic Party—led by post-Civil War forces across the South strongly resisted racial equality, opposing the 13th, 14th, and 15th Amendments and pushing violence against Blacks. Democratic Party racism persisted into the 1960s, after which civil rights legislation which began under Republican President Dwight D. Eisenhower in the 1950s sought to bind wounds, making equality real. Jim Crow laws voter suppression and segregation date to Southern Democrats. Likewise, racist restraints on individual liberties, privileges, and opportunities were driven by Southern Democrats, not Northern Republicans. That legacy is sad, but honest reporting. While racism jumps party lines, willful indifference to history is ignorance. Those who want the truth, must embrace history: Racism flourished under Democrats, not Republicans. The modern Republican Party was founded on the abolition of slavery.

From Abraham Lincoln, Frederick Douglas, and Susan B. Anthony to Dwight Eisenhower, Ronald Reagan, and Donald Trump, Republicans have consistently pushed equality of opportunity, spoken against racism, and advanced equal access to the American Dream—premised on an equal chance at life, liberty, and the pursuit of happiness. Until the advent of a seemingly perpetual "federal entitlement state," created by Democrats in the 1960s and targeted at urban minorities, Republicans were dragging Democratic politicians to the cause of equality. Thus, Lyndon Johnson only signed the 1964 Civil Rights Act after opposing Eisenhower's 1957 and 1960 Civil Rights Acts; Johnson's Senate Democrats filibustered both. On "vote suppression," reality is also different from the modern narrative.

That term is falsely identified with modern state legislation seeking to prevent voting fraud, specifically assuring votes are cast by citizens (as illegal immigration grows), cast and count transparency exists, and practices like "ballot harvesting," out of precinct voting, on-line fraud, and unclean voter rolls end. The goal is simple and clear, restoring public trust in the electoral process. Truth lies elsewhere. Jim Crow laws seeking to block Blacks from voting were a pernicious Democrat invention, one that blocked both Republican and Black voting in the South for more than a century, with the kind of shameless audacity repeated by Senate Democrats who sidelined Black Republican Senator Tim Scott's (R-SC) Comprehensive Police Reform bill in 2020. No excuse justifies that action.

Likewise, major Republican outcomes elevating Black Americans during the tenure of President Trump were underreported. The lowest unemployment rates, highest wage growth, and best economic prospects in 70 years for Black Americans came with Trump's policies. That is not racism; that is anti-racism. That is making the American Dream real for all, true for all.

And for those who say, Eisenhower, Reagan, and Trump were exceptions, or that the economic good times that came to America under their leadership were only coincidentally beneficial for Blacks, that is also untrue. All three aggressively pushed equal advancement, even as they articulated the erosion of dignity that attends federal dependence. Even 1960s Republican presidential candidate Barry Goldwater fought against racial discrimination in his home state. These facts are a matter of historical record and one reason we should not forget history nor tear down that edifice so laboriously built.

The truth is, America is still the land of opportunity, where hard work is rewarded, where most honor liberty and equal opportunity, and where there is a chance to advance. For genuine conservatives, that promise that we are all "created equal" in God's eyes, equally deserving of a right to succeed regardless of skin color has long been an article of faith. Just read the letters of

Lincoln and the works of Russell Kirk, and look at outcomes that followed Ike, Reagan, and Trump. In the end, fiction can be packaged as truth, but it fails. History is our compass. It steers us out of the fog. Genuine conservatives are equitable, honorable, and not racist. Simple, but true. (*AMAC*— Robert B. Charles)

Alert:
Interest on the National Debt, A Monster That is Eating Our Future

We all know government spending is out of control, irresponsible, indefensible. Even now, with the national debt topping $28 trillion, President Biden and congressional Democrats blithely breach their fiduciary and stewardship duties, pushing trillions more in spending. The White House and Congress know our accelerating national debt is "unsustainable." Still they ignore it—and the extraordinary interest that grows on it, shackling America's future. While the national debt itself is sobering, the interest payments on that debt should be scandalizing. Consider that, as Congress and the President continue to increase our national debt, spending with abandon, raising the debt ceiling, adding deficit to deficit, interest on the debt compounds. As interest compounds, it becomes part of the national debt, on which future interest must be paid.

As we borrow more to cover carry-forward debt and compounding interest, borrowing costs of future years are added to what has already accumulated in the past. What does this really mean? It means we are spending money that does not belong to us—money that belongs to our children, their children, and now their children's children. We are literally stealing from the future, financing a spendthrift government that is buying things we do not want with money we do not have, all the while accelerating interest payments. Notably, if inflation continues to rise, the Fed will likely respond by seeking to slow inflation growth with higher interest rates, which means elevated interest on our excessive federal debt—and accrual of even higher interest payments than we already faced. So, as the government borrows to cover debt created by successive deficits, some of that continuous borrowing is for covering the mounting interest.

In sum, we are borrowing and increasing the debt to pay interest on the debt, which creates more debt on which more interest will be due, requiring more borrowing, ad infinitum. Some argue the national debt is not really that important, ostensibly because we are a world leader, a sovereign nation, and our currency's value is based on global confidence in our economic strength. This notion is especially found in Congress, where they seem content to keep raising the debt ceiling, an imaginary limit that keeps getting lifted, now above $28.7 trillion.

At the same time, the Democrat-controlled House and Senate push a $3.5 trillion budget add-on that, as a matter of practice, will also be financed by debt. Is there no shame, limit, chance for self-control, accountability? Equally false is the idea that an economy slowed by middle-class tax hikes, COVID restrictions, elevated regulation, gutting the energy sector, mounting inflation, slowing growth, and higher interest rates will generate revenue sufficient to cover the 2021 deficit, let alone the national debt, or that illusory health care "savings" will miraculously turn the tide or high curl of the debt wave.

A quick look at the national debt should sober every member of Congress; those not sobered by these numbers are drunk on power. The

Congressional Budget Office (CBO) reported in early 2021 that federal public debt—money borrowed from the public—exceeded $21 trillion at 2020's end, equal to 100.1 percent of our Gross Domestic Product (GDP). By the end of July, public debt—a part of our national debt—was 127.65 percent of GDP. Looking ahead, CBO projected that at current rates of growth, the public debt will be more than 200 percent of GDP in 30 years. CBO warned that unrestrained deficit spending and federal debt growth amounts to a "significant risk"—threatening "fiscal crisis," interest payments accompanied by "higher inflation" that will "undermine confidence in the US dollar, making it more costly to finance public and private activity in international markets."

In short, the dollar could plunge, confidence wane, and the US economy—along with all those dependent on public and private sectors—fall flat. Focusing on interest, the lethal effect of compounding interest on our nation's enormous debt can hardly be underestimated. The DC-based Committee for a Responsible Federal Budget (CRFB) advises, "This year, the federal government will spend $300 billion on interest payments on the national debt," which is "the equivalent of nearly 9 percent of all federal revenue collection" or "over $2,400 per household."

Shocking most Americans' expectations, our "federal government spends more on interest than on science, space, and technology; transportation; and education combined," and "the household share of federal interest is larger than average household spending on many typical expenditures, including gas, clothing, education, or personal care." In other words, we are in hock up to our necks, and the level is rising.

The effect of compounding interest on our national debt is hard to express, but by 2028, interest payments will exceed spending on all other major budget categories. Interest on debt will be the largest category of federal spending—made worse by borrowing to cover the interest payments. According to the CRFB, "each one percent rise in the interest rate would increase FY 2021 interest spending by roughly $225 billion at today's debt levels," and "growing debt levels not only add to the likelihood of such increases, but also the cost and risk associated with them." In other words, at a certain point, the tables turn, scale tips, flood tide runs—and we are in trouble. So, taking a deep breath, how do we fix this? Unfortunately, the US Constitution assumes a degree of adult leadership and attention to fiscal responsibility, and contains no amendment mandating a balanced budget, with only loose directives as to how public money is to be managed, today exceeding four trillion tax dollars every year.

The solution lies in setting new limits, putting successive spendthrift Congresses in a fiscal responsibility "box," and putting tax and spend constraints on their behavior. While hard, this increasingly seems one of the only workable ways to impose fiscal accountability; spur entitlement reform; and halt endless deficits, debt, borrowing, and incalculable future interest payments—which will already dog future generations. Solvency must be seen as a national security issue, and Congress must be held to account. One answer widely promoted is a convention of the states, under Article V of the Constitution, which might develop amendments that would work to return solvency, accountability, and sovereignty to the American people.

Any such course would entail risks, and these would need pre-thinking. But inaction in the face of a threat presents its own risks— and debt, interest, and indifference are risks. One way of thinking about an Article V convention might be a Bill of Financial Responsibilities owed to the American people—and made explicit. This idea has been elaborated on by the Reason Foundation, specifically by Senior Fellow John Ramsey, who suggests five elements: simplify taxes; balance the budget; stop excess regulation; create separate and independent trust funds for Social Security Retirement, Social Security Disability Income, and Medicare (with annual audits); and force the federal government to comply with established accounting standards. Seems like common sense, right?

From at least President Reagan forward, Americans have sought to keep their federal government solvent and accountable. As our federal debt, interest payments, borrowing to cover both, and penchant for endless spending hit and hurt, the time has come for insisting on accountability. As individuals, through state legislatures, and by insisting on responsible actions from federal fiduciaries, this is the time to demand accountability. Exponential growth of debt, interest, and borrowing is unsustainable. (*AMAC*—Bob Carlstrom)

Biden Pushing America from Energy Independence to Dependence

On his first day in office, Joe Biden halted construction of the Keystone XL pipeline, jeopardizing the hard-won energy independence secured under President Trump. It was an ominous sign of things to come. Biden has since proceeded to further curtail, and in some cases shut down, American oil production. But even as Biden kills domestic production, he has been forced to pitifully beg for oil from hostile foreign nations. As this article was going to press, Biden was asking OPEC to increase its output. The contrast with President Trump's energy policies could not be any starker. In June of 2017, in a speech at the US Department of Energy, Trump set the tone for US energy policy under his leadership, putting the rest of the world on notice. "My administration will seek not only American energy independence that we've been looking for so long, but American energy dominance," he said.

Trump also predicted the economic boom that would result from cutting-edge hydraulic fracking and horizontal drilling, saying that "we will export American energy all over the world" and that those exports "will create countless jobs for our people, and provide true energy security to our friends, partners, and allies." Trump's remarks reflected his cleareyed view of the reality of the global energy picture as it existed at the beginning of his term, and how energy policy plays a crucial role in ensuring economic and national security. Under Trump's leadership, US oil production skyrocketed from 8.5 million barrels a day in January

2017 to 12.8 million barrels per day by March of 2020. Also true to his prediction, the United States went from being a net importer to a net exporter of oil for the first time since records were kept in 1973. Meanwhile, the US became the world's leader in natural gas production, producing almost all of the natural gas that it consumed.

Trump also ended the Obama administration's misleadingly titled "Clean Power Plan," which would have been catastrophic for the American energy sector. Among other things, the plan pushed the United States to abandon its 250-year supply of coal, leading to the retirement of 546 coal fired power generation units between 2010 and the first quarter of 2019. The results of the Trump America First energy approach were clear across all sectors of the economy. Because of a production boom, the price of natural gas plummeted, making this commodity attractive as a fuel for electricity generation, giving United States electric utilities yet another option to power the grid.

The manufacturing sector, which perhaps benefited most from sound energy policy, added 467,000 new jobs from December 2017 to October 2020. Overall, the industry saw a 3.4 percent increase in employment during the last two years of the Trump administration. According to one study from the American Petroleum Institute, fracking supported 10.3 million jobs near the end of the Trump term. By ending American reliance on foreign oil, the United States also gained a tactical advantage in the war on terror, both by eliminating American reliance on potentially hostile Middle Eastern nations and by stemming the flow of money to the region, where it might be funneled to terror groups. Contrast this focus on energy independence with Biden's bow to the environmental left and complete abdication of American energy leadership in just his first seven months in office.

Biden's cancellation of Keystone XL was just the beginning. The pipeline would've created thousands of jobs and helped cement the energy independence achieved under President Trump. Yet even as he canceled Keystone XL, Biden has removed sanctions on the Russian Nord Stream 2 pipeline, effectively greenlighting a project that even Bob Menendez, the Democrat Chair of the Senate Foreign Relations Committee, called a "bad idea."

After President Trump repealed Obama's Clean Power Plan, he also requested that the Federal Energy Regulatory Commission (FERC) conduct a study on the impact of Democrats' "war on coal" on grid reliability and security. Unfortunately, FERC never completed the study and within weeks of assuming power, Biden's FERC Chairman canceled the study altogether. Biden also ended oil and gas exploration on federal lands in an apparent attempt to appease far-left environmental groups and demanded that his Department of Energy and EPA force the shutdown of even more coal and natural gas power plants by setting a goal of reducing greenhouse gases by 50 percent by 2030—a goal completely detached from reality. In significant part due to Biden's policies, consumers have already been seeing rising energy costs and the highest gas prices in nearly a decade.

Biden's solution, however, has not been to increase domestic production (which he is directly responsible for cutting) but to ask OPEC countries, some of whom have close ties to or are themselves American adversaries, to increase their output, abandoning American energy workers who are still desperately struggling to recover from drastically reduced demand during the COVID-19 pandemic. In short, the Biden administration is rushing headlong toward the failed energy policies of the past. America is once again dependent on hostile nations like Russia for natural gas and Communist China for components needed for the manufacture of "renewables" like solar panels, batteries, and rare earth elements. It will likely only get worse from here if Biden continues to pursue this completely self-inflicted and avoidable energy crisis. In fact, we have already seen the disastrous effects of the Obama-Biden style energy agenda two years ago in Texas, when 4 million Americans lost power during a bitter cold snap that left two hundred dead. The cause?

Too much reliance on subsidized and intermittent renewable energy like wind and solar—exactly the outcome anticipated by the Trump administration and by energy leaders like Jason Isaac at the Texas Public Policy Center, who wrote that "the primary policy blunder that made this crisis possible is the lavish suite of government incentives for wind and solar." Much of the Biden energy policy is justified as being necessary to avert a supposed "climate disaster." Yet even the most ardent supporters of Biden's climate policies confess that total elimination of US emissions won't make a dent in global carbon or global average temperature. Biden's Climate Change Czar, John Kerry, admitted as much this past January, saying, "We could go to zero [net-carbon emissions] tomorrow and it wouldn't make a difference." In fact, the United States is only responsible for approximately 15 percent of the world's carbon emissions. Moreover, US carbon emissions only increased by .04 percent from 1990 to 2019 and decreased 2 percent from 2018 to 2019.

Meanwhile, the Biden administration is incapable of addressing the obvious environmental destruction of the world's actual great polluter, China. The Biden obsession with low carbon energy will cost US citizens hundreds of billions in increased energy costs and replace energy independence with dangerous energy dependence. It will also put the United States at a strategic disadvantage in the global power competition with Russia and China. As those countries continue to develop their energy infrastructure and export capabilities, much of the world, including American allies, will become increasingly reliant on them rather than the United States. President Trump warned that this would occur. During the 2020 campaign, Trump cautioned that "the policies required to implement [Biden's] extreme agenda would mean the death of American prosperity and the end of the American middle class."

Less than one year into his term, Biden has the nation on the road to that dreaded destination of American decline. If his agenda is not stopped, all Americans will suffer. (*AMAC*—Shane Harris)

National Security America Endangered

The Afghanistan catastrophe surfaced all the Biden administration's underlying weaknesses. Here are seven long-term takeaways the US must learn from to avert disaster moving forward.

The events that occurred throughout America's disastrous evacuation of Afghanistan need little elaboration: the Biden administration ceded all control over the country, and even over the fates of American citizens, to the Taliban. The world watched America's longest war end in stunning defeat. Recognizing the Biden administration's weakness, the resurgent Taliban felt empowered to dictate terms to the United States, demanding all US forces leave the country by August 31. Meanwhile, President Biden and senior administration officials, including Secretary of State Antony Blinken and National Security Advisor Jake Sullivan, tried to "spin" one of the worst geopolitical humiliations in US history and ended up acting as de facto propaganda outlets for the Taliban, openly repeating Taliban assurances of "moderation" that flew in the face of the reports of widespread murders and rapes already taking place at the time.

The administration's detachment from reality was so complete that, according to one report from the Washington Post in late August, Taliban leaders, recognizing the chaos engulfing Kabul, offered to let the US military take control of the city and evacuate Americans and other green card holders. Instead, Biden refused to alter his plans and confined the American presence to the Kabul airport. The world watched the crisis that ensued.

We still have much to learn about the failures that got us to this point. Here are seven big take-aways from the Afghanistan disaster that contextualize where we are now and where we must go as America attempts to move beyond this crisis.

1. THE TERRORIST THREAT IS BACK IN A BIG WAY - Twenty years after 9/11, not only do the Taliban control Afghanistan again, but al-Qaeda still exists, and ISIS is resurgent. This is likely a difficult reality for most Americans to acknowledge, particularly after the historic progress made under the Trump administration. Under Trump's leadership, the US military destroyed the ISIS caliphate in Iraq and Syria and killed many high-profile terrorist leaders. When Biden took office, Americans had not heard about a threat from ISIS for years, and a relatively small US footprint in Afghanistan had held the Taliban at bay for more than 18 months without a single American military death. Now, Biden's chaotic retreat and evacuation have reversed that progress and also threatened Trump's other achievements in the region, such as the Abraham Accords. Less than one week after the Taliban took control of Kabul, ISIS fighters killed more than a dozen Americans and hundreds of Afghan civilians in suicide bombing attacks. Some reports have indicated that as much as $85 billion worth of American military hardware is now in enemy hands. At home and abroad, terrorist attacks are on the way, and Americans must prepare for them.

2. THE FAILURE OF US LEADERSHIP HAS EMBOLDENED ALL OF AMERICA'S ADVERSARIES - In the wake of the Afghanistan catastrophe, other geopolitical crises can be expected. North Korea

restarted one of its main nuclear reactors. Iran is looking more recalcitrant. China is moving into Afghanistan to fill the vacuum America left behind. And Taiwan appears under threat like never before. Just days after the Taliban seized control of Kabul, Chinese Communist Party state-run media published an editorial touting the "Afghan abandonment" as a "lesson for Taiwan." The Chinese government has cited the US debacle in Afghanistan as not just a military failure, but a failure of the entire American system of government and way of life. As a result, the Chinese military has increased its activity in the South China Sea, further threatening Taiwanese independence. The message is clear. America's failure in Afghanistan has reinvigorated our enemies and even encouraged them to the point of openly challenging US power in ways previously unimaginable.

3. THE BIDEN ADMINISTRATION'S NATIONAL SECURITY TEAM IS DYSFUNCTIONAL TO THE POINT OF BEING NON-EXISTENT - As Kabul was overrun by Taliban fighters, Biden remained locked away at Camp David, reluctant to address the nation. When he finally did, his remarks amounted to blaming everyone but himself. He repeatedly failed to take questions from reporters, and many public statements from within his administration were contradictory, leading to widespread public confusion and conflicting instructions for those Americans who were still trapped on the ground. Biden's top officials were similarly exposed as out to lunch. Blinken was reportedly vacationing in the Hamptons just hours before Kabul fell. White House Press Secretary Jen Psaki was "out of office" as the Taliban seized the city.

All this from a president who ran on putting the "adults" back in charge. Without competent leadership at the White House, Pentagon, and State Department, the outlook is not good.

4. THE US MILITARY HAS BEEN GRAVELY WEAKENED BY LEADERS THAT PUT WOKENESS AHEAD OF WINNING WARS - Within days of Joe Biden's inauguration, his new defense secretary, Lloyd Austin, announced that climate change would now be considered a top national security priority. Just weeks before the Afghanistan debacle, General Mark Milley, Chairman of the Joint Chiefs of Staff, told a Congressional panel that he wanted to understand "white rage." Around the same time, Chief of Naval Operations Admiral Michael Gilday defended his inclusion of Ibram X. Kendi's How to Be an Antiracist on the Navy's recommended reading list. Among other lies, the book teaches that America is an irredeemably corrupt, evil, and racist nation. Is it any wonder such generals and admirals are losing America's wars? As is always the case, ordinary service members have performed admirably under the circumstances, engaging in heroic acts of courage, kindness, and generosity toward the Afghan people. But those troops' leadership, in both the Pentagon and the White House, has failed them. Preoccupied with chasing phantom enemies like "white rage" and "systemic racism," they have abandoned their central responsibility to protect the country and its allies. Will they be held accountable?

5. A DISASTROUS ADMINISTRATION FOR AMERICA'S ALLIANCES - America's relationship with its allies is at a low point. Joe Biden

abandoned Afghanistan in the middle of the night without any coordination with our NATO partners, putting their lives at risk. As the country was disintegrating, Biden reportedly refused to return the phone calls of the UK's Boris Johnson for days. (Johnson was even rumored to be longing for the leadership of Donald J. Trump.) In a shocking development, the British Parliament voted to hold America's president "in contempt." Armin Laschet, German Chancellor Angela Merkel's heir-apparent, further called Afghanistan "the greatest debacle that NATO has seen since its foundation." French President Macron reportedly phoned Biden with a scathing rebuke. For all the accusations by the media that President Trump would ruin the United States' relationships with its allies, it looks like Joe Biden may actually do it.

6. OUR LIBERAL ELITE IS MORE FOCUSED ON ATTACKING TRUMP SUPPORTERS THAN DEFEATING AMERICA'S ENEMIES - Preposterously, days before the collapse of Afghanistan into a terrorist-controlled hellscape, Biden's Department of Homeland Security issued a bulletin identifying vaccine skeptics and Americans concerned about election integrity as two of the leading terror threats to the United States. When Defense Secretary Austin was confirmed, he didn't talk much about the threat from real terrorist organizations. Instead, he promised to rid the military's ranks of "racists and extremists." Given the lack of evidence that the military has an "extremism" problem, many interpreted this as a signal of a purge of Trump supporters and conservatives from the Armed Forces. Yet, while President Biden bears ultimate responsibility for setting priorities,

there are many who share the blame with him. Congressional Democrats, instead of paying attention to America's defense posture abroad, were busy trying to use the events of January 6 as a cudgel to shame all of the 74 million Americans who voted for President Trump. As a result, they failed to provide any sort of oversight to the Biden administration, only expressing outrage at his plans once it was too late.

7. DESPITE THE NATIONAL SHAME BROUGHT ON BY BIDEN'S FAILED LEADERSHIP, AMERICA REMAINS STRONG - US history is in many ways a cycle of failure followed by national resurgence that leaves the country in an even stronger position than ever before. There is reason to have hope that this pattern will emerge once again now. Most importantly, Americans of all political stripes were rightly horrified at Biden's Afghanistan catastrophe, suggesting that the American spirit remains strong. Biden's support, buoyed in the early months of his presidency by the media's reluctance to cover his many failures, has now taken a significant hit. Most polls currently have Biden's approval rating on Afghanistan sitting somewhere between 20 and 28 percent, almost unheard-of in today's hyper-partisan political climate. As a result, even the mainstream media have started criticizing Biden. Additionally, thanks to President Trump's focus on rebuilding the US military, the country still has the most powerful fighting force in the world, at least when under the right leadership.

Undoubtedly, American national security has been threatened over the past several weeks by President Biden's woeful incompetence and complete lack of leadership. Recovering from this crisis may be years in the making—and it will require a change in leadership in 2022 and 2024 to accomplish it. However, taking stock of where we are now as a nation and what we have learned may just provide some guidance as to how to re-store America's place of prestige among the nations of the world and in the hearts of her own citizens. (*AMAC—Shane Harris*)

Democrats Turn Their Backs on Cuban's Cries for Freedom

The dam may finally break in Cuba. On July 11, tens of thousands of Cubans took to the streets for the first time since the 1990s to try to bring an end to the suffering caused by the communist regime that has ruled their country for more than six decades. Living conditions in the island nation, which were already miserable before, have only been made worse by the COVID-19 pandemic. Families are now deprived of basic goods and services as a result of the economic crisis currently plaguing the island. According to official figures, the Cuban economy contracted nearly 11 percent in 2020. In the first half of 2021, the economy has shrunk another 2 percent when compared to the same time period as last year.

The takeaway is clear communism has once again failed. But not everyone has drawn that logical conclusion. Democrats in Washington have been split in their reaction to Cubans' cries for freedom. On one side, there's an ever-shrinking moderate faction of the party, many of whom are older and understand the dangers of communism and socialism after living through the Cold War. On the other, there is a growing young, radical faction that openly admires Cuba's failed system of government and yearns for socialism to be embraced here in America. Members of the so-called 'Squad' who derive their political beliefs from the Bernie Sanders brand of 'Democratic-Socialism' are the leaders of this movement. The reaction of this younger cadre of radical Democrats to the crisis unfolding in Cuba was predictable, but telling.

Instead of blaming failed socialist policies for the suffering of the Cuban people, left-wing groups who promote progressive causes not only accused America of causing the failures of Cuba's system of government, but also of orchestrating the protests and violence.

Just look at the response of the most prominent organization under the 'Black Lives Matter' umbrella, the Black Lives Matter Global Network Foundation (BLMGNF). The group, whose leaders are self-described Marxists, is extremely influential among the Democrat activist community and helped fuel lawlessness and chaos in cities across the country last summer. Following the unrest in Cuba, the group released a statement that read, "Black Lives Matter condemns the US federal government's inhumane treatment of Cubans, and urges it to immediately lift the economic embargo.

This cruel and inhumane policy, instituted with the explicit intention of destabilizing the country and undermining Cubans' right to choose their own government, is at the heart of Cuba's current crisis." BLMGNF's statement predictably enraged the Cuban-American community, many of whom were quick to point out that the statement parroted talking points used by Cuba's communist regime to defend its continued oppression. One of the most prominent Cuban-American politicians, Florida Senator Marco Rubio, blasted the organization in a tweet: "The extortionist ring known as the Black Lives Matter organization took a break today from shaking down corporations for millions & buying themselves mansions to share their support for the Communist regime in Cuba." Senator Rubio later followed that statement up with a quip that "my office stands ready to help the leaders of the Black Lives Matter organization emigrate to Cuba." Senator Rubio's emphatic statement reflects an emerging dichotomy between the Republican and Democrat Parties in their treatment of Cubans and Hispanics generally that will likely prove electorally consequential in the years to come. Democrats squeaked by last November, but there were legitimate warning signs about how fragile their coalition may be long term.

Pew Research Center's recently released examination of the 2020-electorate documents is likely keeping many Democratic Party officials up at night. One of the key findings of Pew's report details how much President Trump gained amongst Hispanic voters in the 2020 presidential election. "While Biden took a 59% majority of the Hispanic vote, Trump (with 38%) gained significantly over the level of support Republican candidates for the House received in 2018 (25%)." Despite four years of the leftwing media baselessly claiming that President Trump hated Hispanics, the former president received the highest Hispanic vote share for a Republican nominee since George W. Bush's campaign in 2004 and Bush had been governor of Texas.

Former Obama campaign data guru David Shor spoke bluntly about how widespread President Trump's gains with Hispanics truly were in an interview earlier this year: "One important thing about the decline in Hispanic support for Democrats is that it was pretty broad. This isn't just about Cubans in South Florida. It happened in New York and California and Arizona and Texas. Really, we saw large drops all over the country."

Clearly, President Trump's historic economic revitalization, coupled with his fervent anti-socialist message resonated with portions of the Hispanic electorate that were previously reliable Democrat voters. At the same time, Democrats managed to turn off those same voters by embracing socialism, 'wokeness,' and 'defund the police' throughout the 2020 campaign the very same kind of policies that many Hispanics hoped to escape in coming to the United States.

In fact, a recent battleground poll released by the National Republican Senatorial Committee highlighted just how badly the Democrats' socialist agenda is continuing to turn off the key voting bloc. 67 percent of Hispanic battleground voters said capitalism is better because it "gives people the freedom to work and achieve their potential," while only 17 percent said socialism is better because "it is more fair and equitable to working class people."

For years, Democrats clung to the assumption that demographic shifts occurring in the United States would automatically be to their political benefit. But Pew's findings bring that assumption into question. In actuality, the significant trend of Hispanic voters moving toward President Trump could fortify the Republican Party in the years ahead. Some Democrats have recognized the potential disaster for their party if trends seen in 2020 continue, which is why they are trying desperately to flip the script, starting with the crisis in Cuba. Democrat New Jersey Senator and Foreign Relations Chairman Bob Menendez, for example, the son of Cuban immigrants, condemned the Cuban government after last month's protests and implored President Biden and other members of his party to join him. "It is an opportunity for us to change the course of events in Cuba," said Senator Menendez. "If we can help change the course of events in Cuba and give echo to the cries of the Cuban people, that will inure to the benefit of this administration."

Senator Menendez was also one of the few vocal critics in his party of Former President Obama's failed 'Cuban thaw' strategy, which was seen by many as kowtowing to the communist regime. Any Democrat with a shred of political shrewdness would be wise to heed Senator Menendez's advice rather than opting to repeat the mistakes of the Obama era soft-on-Cuba approach. "Squad" leader Rep. Alexandria Ocasio-Cortez, however, is choosing the latter. She was quick to put out a statement in unison with the Black Lives Matter Global Network Foundation also blaming the United States for ongoing Cuban suffering. Rep. Ocasio-Cortez even went a step further and whacked the Biden administration for its reluctance to remove the ongoing embargo of the country almost as if the New York Congresswoman was lobbying directly on behalf of the brutal communist regime.

Increasingly, it appears as if politicians like Menendez are the last remaining vestiges of a 'moderate,' anti-communist, and anti-socialist Democratic Party. The real power center within the ascendant left rests with Ocasio-Cortez' progressive wing, an ominous sign for Hispanic Democrats. The Republican Party should rejoice— they are being handed a golden opportunity to dominate American politics in the decades to come by way of Hispanic voters who refuse to allow the country they love to devolve into the failed systems of government so many of their families escaped. (*AMAC*—Pat Manning)

Top Five Most Harmful Biden Economic Policies

In 2019, the economy hit record numbers across the board, business optimism was high, and business owners were operating in a relatively friendly environment in terms of taxes and regulations. As the current economy continues to recover on shaky footing, President Biden has proposed moving in the opposite direction of the previous administration by dramatically increasing both taxes and regulations on small businesses. President Biden has put forth an ambitious agenda for implementing new spending programs financed by tax hikes, but luckily for the American taxpayer, much of that agenda is currently running into resistance in Congress. Rural state and other moderate Democrats are pushing back against the prospect of taxing small businesses out of existence. Here's a look at the top five most harmful economic policies that have been proposed so far, including a full list of tax hikes being pushed by the Biden administration.

1. Biden's New Double Death Tax

President Trump's signature tax cut legislation, the Tax Cuts and Jobs Act, doubled the exemption for the estate tax, or "death tax," exempting most family businesses and farms, but those changes are set to expire in 2025 if Congress does not act to extend them. President Trump proposed repealing the death tax entirely, but President Biden, according to his FY 2022 budget, has other plans. Biden's budget proposes creating a second death tax on accrued capital gains. That would come on top of (not instead of) the current 40% death tax. A family that has built a mutigenerational business from the ground up and worked their entire lives to grow that business could now be subject to capital gains taxes on the appreciation of that business. Family businesses, farms, and ranches oftentimes appear valuable on paper, but their value is almost entirely tied up in land, equipment, and inventory.

This means when Uncle Sam comes knocking for over 50% of the business upon the death of a business owner, these family businesses are forced to fire workers, sell off equipment, and, in the worst cases, close the doors permanently to pay death taxes.

2. Raising the Top Corporate Tax Rate

The current 21 percent corporate tax rate has put American companies at a significant advantage internationally, but the Biden proposal calls for raising that rate all the way back up to 28 percent. Most economists agree that increasing the corporate rate ultimately falls on the labor market. Americans can expect lower wages and higher prices if the corporate rate is made uncompetitive again. With over 4 million private C-corps in existence today, this tax hike would end up ensnaring small businesses, not just billionaire moguls who have become the poster children for raising corporate taxes.

3. Increasing Regulations and Red Tape

One of President Biden's early executive orders repealed the Trump administration's "two out, one in" rule, which instructed federal agencies to repeal two regulations for every new regulation created. This became an extremely effective way to make sure the government was focused on repealing bad regulations rather than dreaming up new ways to box in small businesses. The previous administration ended up repealing over 8 regulations for every new one created. As is the case on taxes, the Biden administration is pushing hard in the opposite direction, issuing a flurry of new regulations and repealing many of Trump's common-sense directives, like the "two out, one in" rule.

4. Increasing Small Business Audits

President Biden has proposed beefing up tax enforcement in order to squeeze more revenue out of small businesses. In fact, the largest "pay-for" plan in the administration's proposals is to spend $50 billion to close the "tax gap," which they believe will yield over $300 billion for the government. When a small business operating on thin margins has to hire lawyers and accountants in order to comply with aggressive auditing, that means less money for workers and expansion. Recent leaks of personal taxpayer data in order to advance plans to increase taxes are even more reason to cut rather than increase enforcement funding.

5. Increasing Capital Gains Taxes

Over 50 million Americans are invested in the stock market either directly or through their retirement plans. President Biden's plan to hike capital gains all the way up to a top rate of 39.6% for top earners would have a negative effect on the economy and upend retirement plans that depend on dividends. A number of different proposals have been released from the administration and Congressional Democrats on capital gains. Most plans propose, at some level, taxing gains as ordinary income. This means that some taxpayers would lose the preferential treatment of capital gains, which encourages investment and growth. On nearly every front, the Biden administration is looking for more ways to raise revenue in order to finance a multi-trillion-dollar wish list of spending proposals. So far, the Biden administration has proposed hiking taxes in a number of ways in both their "American Jobs Plan" and "American Families Plan."

Now that we've reviewed five of the most harmful policies, here's a comprehensive list of what has been proposed so far.

Biden's American Jobs Plan Tax Increases

• Increase the federal corporate tax rate from 21 percent to 28 percent and tighten inversion regulations
• Raise the tax on Global Intangible Low-Taxed Income (GILTI) to 21 percent, calculate it

on a country-by-country basis, and eliminate the exemption of a 10 percent return on tangible investment abroad (QBAI)

- Impose a 15 percent minimum tax on corporate book income, which would be levied on a firm's financial profits instead of taxable income for firms with a revenue of over $100 million
- Repeal the Foreign-Derived Intangible Income (FDII) deduction, which incentivizes firms to move intellectual property (IP) into the US
- Provide a tax credit for certain onshoring activity and deny expense deductions on jobs that were offshored
- Increase corporate tax enforcement
- Eliminate certain deductions and credits for the fossil fuel industry

Biden's American Families Plan Tax Increases

- Raise the top marginal rate on individuals to 39.6 percent
- Apply ordinary income tax rates to capital gains income of individuals with more than $1 million in taxable income
- Tax unrealized capital gains at death with a $1 million exemption for single filers and a $2 million exemption for joint filers, with additional exemptions for certain types of assets
- Apply the 3.8 percent net investment income tax to all income above $400,000, including active pass-through income
- Make permanent the 2017 tax law's 4639(I) limitation on pass-through businesses' losses

above $250,000 for single filers and $500,000 for joint filers

- Limit 1031 like-kind exchange deferral for gains above $500,000
- Tax carried interest as ordinary income
- Increase individual tax enforcement and enact new reporting requirements for financial institutions Yikes! That's over 15 tax increases just to finance these two plans. As Congress continues to debate the future of Biden's economic proposals, hold on to your wallets, and please join us at AMAC Action as we work to defend America's small businesses from these job-killing tax hikes. (*AMAC*—Palmer Schoening)

Racist? America is Anti-Racist

The more we expect of ourselves—and of each other— the more we harp on missed goals. The key is setting the goal, striving for it, caring about it, self-correcting, and never giving up on the ideal. Racism exists in America, but America is not racist. America may be the least racist nation on the planet, devotedly anti-racist. To divide us by skin color is fundamentally wrong. Before looking at data, ask yourself, what is racism? You do not need a dictionary. It amounts to ingrained prejudice, reflexive judgment, and discrimination based on race, one group toward another. Hardly unique to America, racist tensions appear all over the world—in extremes.

In the Middle East, the Far East, former Soviet Republics, Greater Europe, Africa, and even Central and South America, racism is often cast as a cultural, ethnic, or religious difference, but racism abounds. If children are indifferent to race, adults have warred by tribe since the beginning of time. Racism—disdain and fear of The Other—is innate and must be confronted with the intent to dissolve it, and where in all human history has that been more a mission than in the United States of America? No Chinese, Japanese, Korean, Indian, Arab, African, Russian, German, French, British, or other government has more readily opened its doors, its entire society, to The Other than America. Why? Because even with the challenge of extracting past prejudice, we have never given up the ideal. Whatever our familial, tribal, ethnic, or national origin, we embrace a single idea: Liberty and equality are paramount. These ideals bind us as they bind no other nation. Systemically—yes, let us use that word correctly—these ideals and our attention to them tend to triumph over inborn prejudice based on skin color, origin, and religion, setting the expectation that we will vanquish our divisions, use ideals to animate our decisions, and strive to live as One.

Do we fail? Of course, we do. No great enterprise in human history has been undertaken without failures, backsteps, and resistance, demanding determination, restoration of confidence, resilience, and persistence. Love of liberty and equality is like that.

Reaching higher always empowers the skeptics, critics, and cynics. On our way to the moon, we lost men on the launch pad. On our way to winning World Wars I and II, we had setbacks. Winston Churchill said, "Success is the art of going from failure to failure without loss of enthusiasm." That is our mission today: fending off those who would divide us.

Thus, here are facts which prove America is a beacon, not a burden, a promoter of racial equality and equal protection under law. We have outcomes to prove it. We are not a racist nation but the embodiment of a deep human desire to see liberty and equality live big. Several immutable facts, which are national in character, argue that America is perhaps the most anti-racist nation ever to pursue the goal. We "fail the perfect line," but we never lose sight of it nor our shared constitutional commitment to pursuing liberty, justice, and equal opportunity for all.

Let us start with the basics. America is the most powerful magnet in the world for minorities of all races. "Facts," as Ronald Reagan said, "are stubborn things." America boasts the largest legal immigrant population anywhere, with 40 million citizens born outside the country. We are home to 19 percent of the world's legal immigrants, who make up 13 percent of America's population. Where else is that true? Nowhere. Second, our magnet grows stronger by the decade. Numbers are going up, not down, which would be rather odd for a racist destination. Since 1965, our legal immigrant population has quadrupled. Lest we miss the point, these are legal, law-abiding, assimilating immigrants. Why? Because we are The Other. Name one other country where that is true. Nowhere.

One must ask, if we are racist, why are minorities expending their time and resources, taking risks, and taking a chance with dislocation to seek a visa, become a naturalized citizen, and apply as refugee or asylee? Hispanics, Asians, Africans, Russians, and Europeans come in unrivaled numbers.

Mexico may be the top origin country, but numbers two and three are China and India, and four and five are the Philippines and El Salvador. A full 28 percent of US immigrants hail from Asia, and large swaths are from Europe, Central and South America, the Middle East, and North and Sub-Saharan Africa. Third, African immigrants are seeking visas to America in disproportionately large numbers, which are also rising. Under America's Diversity Visa Program, created by Republican George H.W. Bush in 1990, 38 percent of the 50,000 visas granted in one recent year went to African-born immigrants, the most numerous sub-group since 2013. Fourth, think on another fact: More than half (55 percent) of those coming from Africa are sponsored by an American family (10 percent) or related to an American citizen (45 percent), thus encouraged—not discouraged—to make the effort to seek US citizenship. Fifth, three-fourths of all "out-migration from Africa" to America has occurred after 1990—not before, not in the 1600s, not by slavery, by force, or without legal recourse. Experts say this migration is about rights, opportunities, education, employment, and security—the American Dream. Sixth, once here, immigrants do not pick states by politics, which they would if discrimination marred our map. Thus, the top four destinations are Florida, Texas, New York, and California, two Republican states, two Democrat. Seventh, while African immigrants tend to settle in cities, they migrate over time to suburbs, suggesting income growth, upward mobility, aspirations, and acceptance of differing races.

Eighth, recent polling reinforces how Americans feel about legal immigrants: two-thirds content with current inflow volume, or happy to see more.

Pew Research records most Americans view diversity as positive, and even the Washington Post reports those who grew up in America are more likely to be more tolerant of foreign-born neighbors than in other countries. Ninth, consider what the combination of foregoing facts suggests—that the promise of liberty and equality is real and works for minorities. With a few more stubborn facts, you be the judge. As of 2021, eight of the richest Black billionaires are American, and 25 percent of all American millionaires are Black, Hispanic, or

Asian. Where else in the world is this true? Black Americans own 124,551 American businesses, a third in health care, the highest percentage of any group. Black median income, which fell during Obama's first term, shot up from 2016 to 2019 under Trump before falling to the pandemic—again, a testimonial to equal opportunity.

Nor are opportunities for minorities strictly economic. Roughly 40 percent of the American military is non-white, with opportunities pegged to service, skills, courage, and merit. Where else in the European, Chinese, Russian, Arab, or South American world would you find a Black former National Security Advisor to the President (under Reagan and Obama), Chairman of the Joint Chiefs of Staff (under George H.W. Bush), Secretary of State (twice under George W. Bush), or Secretary of Defense (today), as well as countless Black, Hispanic, and Asian cabinet members (Republican and Democrat)?

Of course, 150 years ago, racism flourished in the South; perverse pockets persisted. But the past is not the present, old is not new, and materiality dies. Even then, 360,000 Union men— almost all white—died to defeat the Confederacy and end slavery, a fact worth remembering. Finally, to punctuate—and rebalance—the national discussion on race and rule of law, consider real numbers around urban police departments, the crucible of the debate.

Los Angeles police are 70 percent minority, Chicago 65 percent, Houston 61 percent, San Antonio 57 percent, Washington DC 65 percent, El Paso 84 percent, and Detroit 61 percent. Where is that reported?

On leading indicia of minority immigration, upward mobility, acceptance, and economic, military, political, and law enforcement advances, America is what we claim and aim to be—a land of individual liberty, opportunity, and equal protection under law. Perhaps the counterproof is best: How many minorities migrate to communist China, autocratic Russia, theocratic Iran, or any other oppressive nation? How many minorities assimilate into Chinese, Russian, European, Arab, African, or South or Central American societies? How many are welcomed by fellow citizens, hired, promoted, admired, or married? How many get rich, invite families, rise in the military, dominate police forces, lead cabinet agencies, advise presidents, or become presidents? Where else in the world but America? Nowhere. These are just facts worth pondering the next time you hear about racism, "Critical Race Theory," and our failings. (AMAC—Robert B. Charles)

Critical Race Theory Seven Hard Truths

Critical race theory (CRT) is all the rage—and causing outrage. This anti-individual, anti-American, fear-focused rebranding of Marxism is now in schools. School boards, afraid of being called racist, are buckling. But parents, grandparents, and students are fighting back. What was once just annoying—pushers of class warfare based on race— is getting personal. As weapons of Marxism show up—name-calling, accusation, intimidation, doxing, firings, suspensions, threats, and violence—reality hits home. America is under fire. The core idea behind CRT is not "equal opportunity" to "life, liberty, and the pursuit of happiness." CRT guts Martin Luther King's dream that Americans "not be judged by the color of their skin, but by the content of their character." CRT despises individualism, such dreams. The goal of CRT is to de-legitimize America, flip the tables on institutions protecting individual liberty, equal opportunity, upward mobility, free-flowing labor and capital, and freedom itself. In place of these constitutional values, CRT aims to reduce us to black and white, incite race warfare, concentrate power, redistribute wealth, and fundamentally remake America. You say, "Whoa—is it that bad?" The answer is—as around the world—yes. But Americans are different. They are standing up to CRT. They are giving voice to seven hard truths:

First, America is about individual equality, not group equity. The idea behind CRT is that America is just groups, defined by skin color. They do not see America as individuals with separate souls, goals, dreams, schemes, skills, hopes, and God-given attributes. Of course, the CRT premise is false. We are born, think, live, dream, and awaken each day as individuals, not groups.

The nation might be divided a million ways—by age, gender, height, weight, hair, eyes, accent, attitude, education, income, geography, health, and, yes, race. But we are individuals. As a self-governing people, we have a constitution that recognizes our individuality, gives us each the same rights under law. Our differences give us separate paths to success, defined by free will. The government's job is to get out of the way, not bulldoze us level. With foresight, our constitution also is self-correcting by amendment. While the first ten amendments came with the articles, others—such as the thirteenth ending slavery, the fourteenth applying equal protection (of individuals) to states, and the nineteenth giving women the vote—came later. So, that is CRT's first lie. Black, white, brown, tan, amber, olive, sallow, bronze, pink, chiffon, baize, or none of the above, we have individual rights— no "group equity" in our constitution.

Second, equal opportunity is not an equal outcome. The constitution, as amended, gives all Americans an equal shot. If we fail to reach perfection, the goal is to keep trying—an equal shot at education, employment, property ownership, returns, and resilience. The goal is equal protection, the right to rise or fall, to succeed, fail and try again—equal under the law. This is the opposite of CRT's guaranteed outcome, materially leveling by group. The idea behind CRT is concentrating power to equalize outcomes, regardless of who earned what. Returns on hard work and trust in the individual are gone.

Third, CRT is itself racist. CRT not only assigns all life grievances by one race to another. It suggests black and white citizens with equal education, employment, ideas, industry, and effort cannot attain similar outcomes. Why? Because the principle of merit based achievement is rejected in favor of reverse racism. Easier to hate and blame than love and support. That approach is anti-American, ironically rife with racial putdown.

Rather than faith in the possible and the individual, CRT defines the possible as impossible—and blames that on race. For the CRT crowd, race is all that matters, pitting one against another, teaching the assumption that we are not equal in God's eyes or the eyes of the law, and never can be in each other's eyes. Have you ever heard of anything more pathetic than teaching children resentment, blame, and hopelessness? In CRT's world, an elite equalizes outcomes by race, killing the American Dream.

Fourth, CRT denies upward mobility. CRT denies the idea that hard work and equal protection succeed. Upward mobility is the gaping hole in Marx's bucket, draining it of power. Put differently, to believe in CRT, you must believe your skin color defines your ability to succeed. If you believe that, you buy into the lie. Ask someone like Colin Powell, who became a four-star general, chairman of the Joint Chiefs, secretary of state and lived the American Dream.

Fifth, CRT immorally pushes intergenerational guilt. It is a fraud because the only way to justify putting one race down for another and openly teaching resentment is to pin the past on the present. The premise is wrong. Intentional infliction of intergenerational guilt, making successors responsible for ancestors, is fundamentally immoral. Morality centers on individual accountability, not accountability for distant progenitors. Must a newborn Japanese baby pay for Tojo's horrors? A newly born German baby account for Hitler? Is moral accounting due for cross-enslavement by three thousand African tribes? Is modern Turkey responsible for the Ottoman enslavement of Eastern Europeans? The point is we have individual sovereignty under natural, constitutional, and statute law; every life is sacred and belongs to itself. Consider Ezekiel 18:20: "The child shall not share the guilt of the parent." How much more so a great-great-great-grandparent? And intergenerational debts, called "peonage" or "debt slavery," are illegal. To resuscitate such concepts in the service of CRT and resentment is immoral.

Sixth, CRT empowers elites to persecute. Every Marxist country in the world, every country that has ever picked a racial, ethnic, religious, or economic group to blame for society's ills, has done so by empowering an elite to push mass persecution. That is not America, but where CRT leads.

Seventh, CRT ignores data. Perhaps the biggest lie in CRT is that America is racist. No country in the world attracts more minorities than America. We are the magnet, with the largest immigrant population in the world, forty million Americans born elsewhere—most minorities, many African. By wealth, Black, Hispanic, and Asian Americans account for 25 percent of America's millionaires—proving the American Dream, upward mobility, and capitalism. And Pew Research reports most Americans see racial diversity as good. So much for CRT. In the end, CRT is Marxism, pushing resentment, blame, guilt, fear, silence, and compliance. Do not buy it. Americans cleave by values, not skin color. Critical race theory is junk—a disgrace. (*AMAC*—Robert B. Charles)

Seven Patterns Now Shaping the 2022 Midterms

A s Congress readies itself for the August recess, the political landscape has already transformed from the seemingly dire conditions for Republicans last winter. As we head toward the fall, the troubled terrain facing Democrats ahead is becoming clearer by the day. Here are the 7 developments that will define the remainder of 2021, and most likely the midterms next year.

Biden is No Moderate.

For many Americans—and likely most of President Biden's voters— the one and only reason Joe Biden's candidacy was appealing was his signature promise to govern moderately, resist the radical left, and steer the country back to the center. "Do I look like a radical socialist?" Biden asked last summer, in an attempt to distance himself from his party's most extreme voices. This promised approach to policymaking, however, has not been reflected in his administration's first six months.

Thus far in his presidency, Biden has promoted packing the Supreme Court, abolishing the filibuster, abolishing voter ID, and undermining religious liberty protections, among a host of other extremely controversial policies. In the wake of Biden's march to the left, prominent Democrat voices have sounded the alarm. Democratic consultant James Carville stated that "Wokeness is a problem and we all know it." Commentator Andrew Sullivan similarly expressed shock that

President Biden has introduced "the most brazenly leftist, spend and borrow agenda of any president resident" in decades.

Most alarmingly for Democrats, a Media Research Center report found that when Biden's voters are presented with Biden's real policy priorities, one in six, or 17 percent, say they regret their decision to vote for him. The mismatch between what voters were promised and what they are receiving is bound to result in a growing backlash.

The Border Disaster

Perhaps no contrast between President Trump's and President Biden's policies is clearer than their approaches to border security. As Trump points out, when he left office, illegal border crossings had been cut by as much as 90 percent. After Biden abolished most of Trump's border security and immigration enforcement measures, the border crisis began almost immediately. The country appears on track to see roughly 2 million people cross the border illegally this year—a surge of staggering proportions. A June Harvard/Harris poll found that 80 percent of registered voters think illegal immigration is a serious problem. Furthermore, the survey finds that a sizeable majority of voters think the Trump administration's immigration policies should have been left in place. What will happen in the fall as the crisis continues to worsen—and how can Biden do anything to address it that does not provoke a rebellion from the left?

Soaring Inflation

Under Biden, inflation has now reached its highest level in 13 years, and Americans are noticing. The price of everything from gasoline to food to building materials is skyrocketing. In addition to the $1.9 trillion in spending that he signed into law, Biden is already pushing for trillions more, which is likely to fan the inflationary flames even further.

A Monmouth University poll shows that 71 percent of Americans are now worried that Biden's spending plans will lead to more inflation—a remarkable number for an issue that was not even on the radar last fall. Again, it is unclear what Biden can do to address this growing concern.

Biden Weakness on the World Stage

From easing sanctions on Iran to allowing China to mock "American-style democracy" on US soil, Biden's foreign policy has been a naked display of American weakness. His trip to the G7 was a debacle in which his administration insulted the British, our closest ally. Days later, in Biden's media appearance following a summit with Russian President Vladimir Putin, Biden made no mentions of sanctions against Moscow, Russia's reliance upon the use of chemical weapons in Europe, or the 2018 poisonings in Salisbury, England of a former Russian military intelligence officer and his daughter. Rather than imposing additional sanctions on Russia in the weeks leading up to the summit, Biden lifted sanctions on the Nord Stream 2 pipeline giving Russia the capability to put the squeeze on our European allies whenever it wants by stopping the shipment of vital natural gas. One such event does not gravely damage a president or his party. Many such event leave an indelible impression in the minds of the American People.

The Alarming Crime Wave

With a deliberate departure from the Trump administration's law and order approach, crime has sharply increased under the first months of the Biden presidency. The murder rate has just seen its largest single year increase in history, and carjackings are becoming commonplace in cities nationwide.

While Democrats continue to push for far-reaching anti-police legislation and many progressives continue their calls to defund the police, six in 10 Americans view crime as a major issue. As crime continues to increase at a nearly unprecedented rate, more Americans are seeing the root causes as having to do with President Biden and the Democrats.

Yet again, Biden's left flank leaves him with little leeway to meaningfully address the problem. All he can talk about is gun control—the last thing Americans want when faced with a surge in violent crime.

Democrats Have Become the Party of Critical Race Theory

In March, Biden's Department of Education proposed a rule to give the federal government the power to coerce schools nationwide into teaching Critical Race Theory (CRT), a Marxist-inspired ideology that pits groups against each other based on skin color. Believing that all of human history and social identity ought to be viewed through a racial lens, this ideology is now wholly embraced by the Democrat party while its leftwing allies are spreading it rapidly through our nation's classrooms and even the military. The American people are not buying it. A June poll conducted in battleground states found that independents reject CRT by an overwhelming 76 percent to 20 percent. 22 states have either introduced or signed into law legislation that prohibits CRT from being taught in public schools, and the grassroots opposition to CRT is growing. How can Democrats pivot away from such lunacy without devolving into a civil war among themselves?

Donald J. Trump is Back and Getting Stronger

Perhaps the most surprising, and also the most important, political development of this year has been the remarkable return of former President Trump to center stage. In the immediate aftermath of the 2020 presidential election and the events of January 6, some said that Trump was destined to retire to Florida and fade from political attention. Yet he has defied those expectations and clearly remains a potent—perhaps the most potent—force in American politics. Over the summer, Trump has resumed his trademark rallies, attracting tens of thousands of people. This sets Trump up to be the loudest and most formidable critic of Biden and the Democrats going into the midterms.

Another pattern fueling President Trump's increasing strength is the media's gradual—and reluctant— acknowledgement that President Trump was right about many things the media once vociferously declared to be untrue. As Trump recently put it in a statement, since he left office they have conceded that COVID-19 likely emerged from a Chinese lab, hydroxychloroquine works, Lafayette Square was not in fact vacated for a photo op during last summer's riots, Hunter's laptop was real, the "Russian Bounties" story was a hoax, the Mueller investigation showed no collusion, the vaccines were indeed produced by the end of 2020 just as Trump predicted, borders in fact are necessary, Critical Race Theory is indeed a disaster, schools should in fact have been opened much earlier just as Trump had said, and lockdowns did not actually work to contain the virus. In short, Trump was right and Biden and the media were wrong about a growing list of issues.

The Year Ahead

As the American people continue to recognize these and other emerging patterns, opposition to the agenda of President Biden and his left-wing allies will likely grow. As a result, when Congressional Democrats return from recess in

September, they may find they have not much momentum to pass their most prized legislative priorities— like the Equality Act, voting "reforms," and the radical social transformation plan contained in their so-called infrastructure bill. Biden and the Democrats will then be at a crossroads: will they heed the interests and values of the American people, who by and large do not want such left-wing extremism, or will they continue to bow down to the wishes of their most left-wing members and plunge ahead?

And a still more pressing question for Biden and the Democrats: is it even possible for them to rebrand themselves as moderates after the image of extremism that their rhetoric and record have by now imprinted on the public? The answer will likely determine the control of Congress a little more than one year from now. (*AMAC*—Seamus Brennan)

The 1619 Project

In August 2019, The New York Times came out with this paragraph on the cover of its companion periodical, The New York Times Magazine: "In August of 1619, a ship appeared on this horizon, near Point Comfort, a coastal port in the British colony of Virginia. It carried more than 20 enslaved Africans, who were sold to colonists. America was not yet America, but this was the moment it began." It was surely news to many Americans that our country began in 1619. The pilgrims' landing on the Mayflower in 1620 in Massachusetts or the Declaration of Independence of 1776 are the traditional dates we associate with America's founding, with our national holiday of July 4 celebrating the latter, of course.

The principal author of the project was Nikole Hannah-Jones, and the timing of her work was intentional to coincide with the 400th anniversary of the first enslaved Africans arriving in the Virginia colony. The project made news and headlines after its publication and again in May 2020 when the project creator won the Pulitzer Prize for Commentary. The 1619 Project gained additional attention after the looting and rioting of the summer of 2020 that followed George Floyd's death. If it had only been an exposé on the state of race relations in America, always an important topic ripe for healthy debate among liberals and conservatives in our society, then perhaps little hullabaloo might have followed. But no. One sentence in particular stirred a hornet's nest of controversy, and not merely from conservatives.

A number of prominent liberal academics felt obliged to weigh in on Hannah-Jones's most contentious claim: "One critical reason that the colonists declared their independence from Britain was because they wanted to protect the institution of slavery in the colonies, which had produced tremendous wealth." Leslie M. Harris, a professor of history at Northwestern University, was tasked with fact-checking the piece— in advance.

Harris advised against publishing that statement. When ignored, she later explained her criticism of the project and The Times in a March 2020 op-ed in Politico, entitled, "I Helped Fact-Check the 1619 Project. The Times Ignored Me."

Even the most amateur student of history would recall that the American Revolution had as its origins in the rallying cry of "no taxation without representation." Great Britain was levying taxes without any input from the colonists in America, who were obliged to pay them. The tax on tea, enjoyed by much of the population, was particularly scorned and led to the famous Boston Tea Party, two years before the first shots were fired at Lexington and Concord. Slavery, while indeed present in every colony, was not the issue. As Harris wrote in her op-ed, "Slavery in the colonies faced no immediate threat from Great Britain, so colonists wouldn't have needed to secede to protect it."

Princeton historian Sean Wilentz accused the 1619 Project of "cynicism" and led a successful effort to bring four prominent scholars in the field to take the highly unprecedented step of signing a letter rebuking it. The very stature of the four— James McPherson, Victoria Bynum, Gordon

Wood, and James Oakes—called into question the credibility of the entire project. Journalist Andrew Sullivan's September 2019 op-ed, entitled, "The New York Times Has Abandoned Liberalism for Activism," took strong aim at a different introductory sentence by Hannah-Jones: "Our democracy's ideals were false when they were written."

It is noteworthy that the most hotly contested sentence was eventually modified to "some of the colonists fought to preserve slavery" in response to criticism. Many liberals lament that a single sentence caused such a distraction from a piece they otherwise liked and highly praised.

Adam Serwer of The Atlantic argues the fight over the 1619 Project is more about vision than facts. Think of it as the pessimists versus the optimists. The pessimists take a dark view of America and its future, where blacks forever struggle for rights that will never be achieved. When Hannah Jones wrote "anti-black racism runs in the very DNA of the country," James Oakes, a signatory to the infamous rebuke letter, said, "The worst thing about [this view] is that it leads to political paralysis [...] There's nothing we can do to get out of it. If it's in the DNA, there's nothing you can do. What do you do? Alter your DNA?" Think of it. If America is so inherently racist to its core that people cannot grow or change over time, why bother trying?

Even education itself would be useless and society fated to be racist forever. Naturally, some on the political left and most on the right disagree with this assessment. Optimists of both political stripes take the long road, praising how far

America has come since the American Revolution and even in the last few decades.

Where do things stand now? The latest fight appears to be over the 1619 Project curriculum, a series of lesson plans, activities, guides, and resources for teachers to use in the classroom. The American Revolution Institute describes the curriculum as "actually worse than the dishonest and deceptive material on which it is based" and adds "the premise of the curriculum is that Hannah-Jones has discovered a fundamental truth about American history that has eluded the historical profession: that the central, defining feature of American history and culture is racism."

What have political leaders said about the project? Not surprisingly, then-Senator Kamala Harris praised the project in a tweet, saying it "is a powerful and necessary reckoning of our history."

Former House Speaker Newt Gingrich criticized the project as "brainwashing" and, in an op-ed, characterized it as "left-wing propaganda masquerading as 'the truth.'"

No one has been more outspoken, however, than Senator Tom Cotton (R-AR). His press release of July 2020 labeled the project "a racially divisive, revisionist account of history that denies the noble principles of freedom and equality on which our nation was founded. Not a single cent of federal funding should go to indoctrinate young Americans with this left-wing garbage." Cotton followed by introducing the "Saving American History Project of 2020."

With the Biden administration now in charge of federal education policy, it remains to be seen what influence the 1619 Project will have in K-12 classrooms in the future. Minority Leader Mitch McConnell sent a letter to Education Secretary Miguel Cardona on April 30, 2021, protesting a proposal to incentivize the use of the project through federal grants. McConnell noted "actual trained, credentialed historians with diverse political views have debunked the project's many factual and historical errors." Together with critical race theory, wokeness, and cancel culture, parents and patriots alike will have to monitor their local school curricula carefully. (*AMAC* — Jeff Szymanski)

CHAPTER THREE
Champion of Freedom of Religion

PRESIDENT TRUMP HAS ALWAYS BEEN PRO-
life. President Biden has been pro-choice ever since he rejected the Hyde Amendment, which protected viable unborn babies. He did so for political gain with pro-choice women who demanded legal abortion to the point of infanticide. He curried favor from the left-wing Planned Parenthood supporters. Biden is a Catholic in name only. Church teaching is that personhood commences from conception to natural death. You will never find the words *fetus* or *blob of tissue* in a Catholic catechism or Christian Bible. "Before I formed you in the womb, I knew you, and before you were born I consecrated you. I have appointed you a prophet to the nations" (Jeremiah 1:5). Jeremiah was set apart for his prophetic mission before he was born. This verse confirms that personhood begins with conception. Therefore, unborn children who are aborted have been denied God's mission for them.

In 1973, the US Supreme Court decided that a woman had a

constitutional right to have an abortion (*Roe v. Wade*). Nineteen seventy-three was a pivotal year in degrading American culture. The right of a mother to murder her unborn child is the ultimate of violence. Saint Mother Teresa decreed abortion as the cause of nuclear war. The transformation of the United States, a nation founded on the Judeo-Christian ethos, to a secular irreligious one is well underway. The 1960s revolution (sex, drugs, rock and roll) was the inception of a new culture for present-day millennials who disavowed traditional family values and the nuclear family, as well as the role of religion and affirmation of God.

Forty percent of pregnant women will become single-parent mothers; they will be divorced or never married. The breakdown of the family has left millions of children with no fathers in the home. Unless this trend is reversed, millions of kids will become juvenile delinquents, drug abusers, and godless. Unless there is a spiritual awakening that Mike Evans predicts in his book *The Coming of the Great Awakening*, repentance for our mad depravity, the United States is doomed. I pray for the babies being born today who will grow up in an atheistic, socialist, or communist country, perhaps an ally and tributary of the People's Republic of China. Don't think this is farfetched.

The US Supreme Court banned prayer in public schools in 1962 in a case known as *Engel v. Vitale*. The full text of the twenty-three-word prayer was "Almighty God, we acknowledge our dependence upon Thee, and we beg Thy blessings upon us, our parents, our teachers and our Country. Amen." The court ruled that the Board of Regents prayer was a violation of the Constitution Establishment Clause, which precluded our country from ever forming a state religion. The truth is that the prayer reflected no particular religion and was voluntary. The court majority held that, because the prayer did not address the belief of atheists, it violates the Establishment Clause. The truth is that for 170 years after the ratification of the Constitution and Bill of Rights, no court had ever struck down any prayer, in any form, in any location. The atheists won the day. We should be cognizant that atheists hate religion and especially the Bible. I fear that someday in a socialist or communist "United Socialist States of America," religion will be banished. In fact, I suspect that socialists will ban reading the Bible, and it will be a crime as it is today in Saudi Arabia. The Muslims refer to the Christians and Jews as infidels, but at least they have a strong belief in God.

Let me make this clear. The Muslim religion is closely related to the Christian and Jewish faiths. The Koran, as revealed to Mohamed, includes Jesus and Moses as great prophets. The Muslim, Christian, and Jewish faiths adhere to one God as revealed to Abraham, the founder of Judaism. Judaism introduced monotheism (belief in one God) to the world. The Christian faith was built on the Jewish faith, and Islam was built on both. The sacred scriptures of these religions all command daily prayer to God and charity to people in need. There have been sectarian wars among these religions. Catholics and Protestants who claim to be Christians killed one another for hundreds of years. Sunnis and Shia killed one another for hundreds of years, and yet they are Muslim sects. The faiths are peaceful, albeit many of their adherents are not. Why not? It is the carnal nature of people to be martial. That is why people kill one another in wars. Our violent natures are restrained by the peace sought by our religions. However, people who are atheists do not believe in God or religion. They are not constrained by the stricture of scripture.

Karl Marx was an atheist who founded the false religion of communism, which preaches that since there is no God or religion, people must rely on themselves to be peaceful. Foolishly, they believe people will make this a better world through the communist manifesto written by an atheist, Karl Marx. He was the champion of secular humanists who still believe that we can improve this world without having God-centered lives. The result has been totalitarian governments—communist countries such as the Union of Soviet Socialist Republics, which has collapsed and been replaced by the Russian Orthodox Church, which is Christian. Other parts of the former Soviet Union are now republics, mostly Muslim. Today, the biggest threat to world peace is the People's Republic of China, whose official religion is atheism, espoused by 90 million atheists of the Chinese Communist Party (CCP). The sole leader of China, president for life, is atheist Xi Jinping, who is the dictator of one and a half billion Chinese people.

He brooks no dissent of anyone and does not respect human rights. All religious liberty is repressed. Christians and Muslims are under surveillance. One million Muslim peaceful Uyghurs are in detention camps, and the residents of Hong Kong have been denied freedom of speech, breaking a ninety-nine-year treaty with Great Britain that guaranteed their freedom of speech and press. I will write more about China in the next chapter.

In the United States, President Thomas Jefferson wrote that the very Declaration of Independence should make no legislature allowed to make a law expecting an establishment of religion or prohibiting the free exercise thereof, thus building a wall of separation between church and state. In effect, the Declaration of Independence and the Constitution guarantee the freedom of religion by the choice of the people. Obviously, Jefferson did not see a nonsectarian working of God as an establishment of religion. Therefore, a tiny atheist segment of the American people cannot foist their will on the vast majority of the American people who have a right to pray in any location, in a nonsectarian way, and that includes American public schools. In history, both houses of Congress always open with a prayer. The Supreme Court opens with "God save The United States and their Honorable Court." Our money is stamped "In God We Trust," but God cannot be involved in any public school in America. This is sheer hypocrisy. Christians, Jews, Muslims, and all religious persons should reject this overly blatant attack on religion.

This disgrace is applauded by atheists, socialists, and communists. I pray that the majority justices of the Supreme Court are never atheists. I pray that the present majority conservative justices repeal the abominable *Roe v. Wade*. Let the states decide the extent of a woman's reproductive rights. Remember, the fact of abortion invades the right of privacy since the woman, doctor, attendants, and the unborn child are present.

Planned Parenthood should not be funded by taxpayer dollars. There is always an alternative to abortion—for example, adoption by married couples who are eager to share their love with unwanted children. The legalizing of abortion in 1973 was not the first unjust law in our history. The absolute truth is that unjust laws are not laws at all. I beseech you to read *Dark Agenda, the War to Destroy Christian America*, written by David Horowitz, a noted conservative Jew.

As of this writing, Joe Biden has reversed nearly all of Trump's accomplishments. He has rejoined the Paris Climate Treaty, which will cost the US the greatest part of its budget, whereas China bears no expense and does not reduce its carbon emissions until 2030. Under Trump, we became the largest oil producer in the world; we were energy independent. The radical Democrats want to implement the Green New Deal, using the sun and wind for our energy needs. When it rains, the solar panels don't work. On windless days, the windmills don't work unless electricity generates them. Oil is needed for turbines. These alternative energy sources account for supplying 10 percent of our energy requirements. The cost of the Green New Deal will be $50–100 trillion over the next twenty years. Joe Biden has rejoined the Trans-Pacific Partnership, which will result in massive job losses to China. Biden wants to renew Obama's treaty with Iran, eliminating all sanctions on Iran. Of course, Iran is allowed to make money to build a nuclear bomb by producing more oil. Biden has lifted the terrorist label on Iran-backed groups that are terrorists (Hamas, Hezbollah, Houthi, et al.) and cut off weapons to allies fighting them.

I must include David Horowitz's cogent article on the First Amendment and free speech in our book: David Horowitz is a timely prophet. He prophesied,

For the first time in our lives, free speech is about to be criminalized. We never thought this day would arrive in America. Last year, we learned that they can shout "COVID" as an emergency, and our life, liberty, and property disappear. They can shout "racism" and our inalienable right to self-defense disappears. The last thing we had was the freedom to criticize what is happening, even if there was nothing we can do about it. Now they can shout "right-wing terrorism" or "right-wing conspiracy" and say that freedom of speech no longer applies.

Leftists in this country claim that their violence is speech and our speech is violence. That is why they glorified riots last year that burned down numerous cities, caused thousands of injuries, cost billions of dollars, and elevated their cause as the most urgent grievance in need of redress. At the same time, they are pushing to criminalize not just the violent actors and actors of the Capitol on January 6th, but any view or speech or assembly predicated on views that are held by those people.

This is why they seem to be taking direct shots at The First Amendments' guarantee of freedom of speech for Americans, even as they plan amnesty to those whose entire presence in this country is illegal or everyone focuses on the corporate world violating the spirit of The First Amendment by excommunicating anyone with conservative views, but the government has a monopoly on violence, law, and the ability to restrain our liberty. If we don't wake up immediately, our speech and freedom to assemble will not only be censored, but criminalized. It started on January 6th, when Tom Edsall published a column in The New York Times noting, "A debate has broken out over whether the once-sacrament constitutional protection of The First Amendment has become a threat to democracy."

This is a tried and trusted tactic of the left—to have columnists flout a radical idea as a "debate" while their governmental actors begin working on it in earnest.

Just take stock of what we are seeing out in the open. They are now arresting people all over the county for merely being in the Capitol, even if they didn't engage in violence, vandalism, or theft. Had this standard been applied to Black Lives Matter, there would literally have been millions of arrests. So no, this is not just about punishing those who acted violently. The FBI is placing signs all over the country asking people to report those who were at the Capitol, something that never happened even in the most deadly Black Lives Matter/Antifa riots last year, or at Trump's inauguration years ago in D.C. They are militarizing D.C. with 20,000 troops when the threat of violence against Trump's inaugural guests four years ago was exponentially greater. They are declaring emergencies in states as remote as New Mexico with no evidence of violence present. Garrett Soldano, a leader in the anti-lockdown movement in Michigan, claims the FBI paid him a two hour visit because a local called the FBI and claimed he is a violent extremist.

The FBI had done this when hundreds of buildings were on fire for days on end with no control among the local police departments, I would just feel that they are being overly cautious. Given that Black Lives Matter was promoted as the leader of our civic discourse and we are all being treated like terrorists, however, we should be very scared they are coming for The First Amendment, not for national security. Remember, the Justice Department seems to believe this was a planned attack. So the hundreds of thousands of Trump supporters who just came there to express their views had no idea that a few bad actors were planning this.

Last week, Pennsylvania's Lieutenant Governor, John Fetterman, said emphatically that The First Amendment doesn't apply to sentiments he doesn't agree with. "This idea that saying that Pennsylvania was "rigged" or that we were "trying to steal the election." - That's a lie. And you do not have the right, that is, not protected speech."

Thus, from now on, Democrats can unilaterally change election law in the middle of an election—up until and abolishing Election Day in favor of mail-in ballots—and anyone who criticizes it or organizes a rally against it is subject to prosecution? These comments would be comical if they didn't coincide with actions taken by his party coming into power in Washington that look a lot like martial law. In other words, if you watch the language the left is using about our speech and the actions the Biden administration and the governors are taking, it's quite evident that Big Tech is not the only thing we have to worry about. If nothing changes, I predict that even Parlor is able to become completely independent in the private market, the government, which has the ultimate monopoly on power, will shut it down.

Last week, Minnesota Attorney General Keith Ellison, the same man who is prosecuting business owners and threatening them with labor camps for earning a living, said on a conference call with prosecutors that he is investigating those from his state who merely attended the rally.

Already in 2019, Richard Stengel, the Biden transition "team lead" for the U.S. Agency for Global Media, wrote in a Washington Post op-ed that The First Amendment needs curtailment. "All speech is not equal. And where truth cannot drive out lies, we must add new guardrails. I'm all for protecting thought that we hate, but not speech that incites hate." Wrote Stengel. This is pretty bizarre coming from a side of politics that already controls 99 percent of all speech and big business that controls speech. What exactly are they afraid of? If anything, we are the ones who should be scared of their speech, given the monopoly they hold.

Well, George Washington already warned us about the motivations of those who clamp down on speech. "For if men are to be precluded from offering their sentiments on a matter, which may allow the most serious and alarming consequences, that can invite the consideration of mankind, reason is of no use to us. The freedom of speech may be taken away, and dumb and silent we may be led, like sheep, to the slaughter," said Washington in an address to The Continental Army on March 15, 1783.

The question facing patriots in the coming days is quite simply this: Will we allow that final domino to fall? The Democrats have impeached Donald Trump twice. The first time, the first days of his term in office, the Democrats sought to impeach Trump. The House, under Nancy Pelosi, accusing him of collusion with Russia and obstruction of justice. They had majority numbers in the House so they succeeded. After four years of investigation by special prosecutor, Robert Muller, and 30 plus millions of taxpayer money, there was no evidence of collusion nor obstruction of justice, so there was no trial in the Senate. President Trump was not distracted from implementing his celebrated policy goals. Lower taxes for the public and corporations; lower capital gains taxes for individuals and corporations; the highest employment levels in history, and 3 to 4 percent gains in Gross Domestic Product (GDP) which is the measurement of the value of goods and services produced. Trump infuriated the Democrats (elected officials and private citizens) by defeating them. Their hatred of him is intense. The majority Democrats in the House succeeded in impeaching Trump a second time for inciting a riot on the Capitol on January 6th, 2021. This time he was subjected to a sham trial which was unconstitutional since he was not a sitting president nor was a Supreme Court justice presiding. Of course, Donald Trump was acquitted, and he is eligible to run for president in 2024! Alleluia!

Back-to-Back Impeachment Champ

Here is an analogy of the Democrats' bouts of impeachment against Donald Trump. They lost the first bout of boxing because there was no evidence of collusion of Trump with Russia or his obstruction of justice. They lost the second bout because of their sham trial of Trump in the Senate (the Constitution stipulates on the impeachment of a sitting president and a Supreme Court justice for said trial), so they lost the conviction of Donald Trump. In boxing terms, Donald Trump won both matches. Donald Trump's record as president: Two victories and no losses (2–0). Therefore, Donald Trump is a champ in back-to-back impeachments. If he takes on the Democrats again in 2024, I bet he will be victorious!

The Democrats should be ashamed of themselves for wasting time and taxpayer money. Instead, they should be working with Republicans on increasing jobs, immigration reform, bolstering our military and police, and improving our infrastructure. President Biden is not addressing these crucial issues. In his campaign, he called for unity. Thus far, he has issued more executive orders than Trump, Obama, and Bush combined. Why is he ruling the country with no consent of the Congress?

The World Health Organization (WHO) is no friend of the United States. They were well aware that COVID-19 was transmissible from human to human long before they announced this truth to the world. In order to curry favor and money from China, they reported that the Wuhan laboratory did not manufacture it. President Trump withdrew the United States from this dishonest organization. President Biden has issued an executive order for Americans to refer to the deadly virus as COVID-19, not the "China virus," even though it originated in China. Of course, the World Health Organization now denies that this plague originated in China.

The United States has suffered 960,000 deaths so far with twenty-nine million Americans contracting this deadly disease. Thank God, a vaccine was developed under Trump and is currently being distributed throughout the US and the world.

In my opinion, Ron DeSantis, Republican governor of Florida, would make an excellent vice president when Donald Trump runs for president in 2024. Ron DeSantis received a BA from Yale University and a JD from Harvard Law School. He joined the US Navy from 2004 to 2010, serving as a judge advocate general officer advising troops in Iraq and at Guantanamo Bay. DeSantis became a memory of the US Navy Reserve following his active duty service and worked as a federal prosecutor.

Before his election as governor, DeSantis was elected to three terms in the House of Representatives. He resigned his House seat in 2018 to campaign for governor. When he was a member of the House, he was a founding member of the conservative House of Freedom Caucus. He sponsored amendments to institute term limits for members of Congress.

DeSantis said the following of the 2017 amendment, which he introduced with Senator Ted Cruz, Republican from Texas: "Term limits are the first step toward reforming Capitol Hill. Eliminating the political elite and infusing Washington with new blood will restore the citizen legislature that our Founding Fathers envisioned. The American people have called for increased accountability and we must deliver."

As Governor of Florida, he opposes tax increases, ending Common Core, and prohibiting sanctuary cities in Florida. DeSantis refuses to shut down businesses during the pandemic because he doesn't want to ruin Florida's booming economy. DeSantis describes himself as a "conservative in the Reagan tradition."

In my opinion, Ted Cruz, Republican senator of Texas, would make an excellent vice president when Donald Trump runs for president in 2024. Ted Cruz is a conservative proponent of limited government, economic growth, and the strict interpretation of the Constitution.

After being tortured and imprisoned in Cuba, Ted's father, Rafael, fled to the US. He is now a pastor in Dallas. Ted's father recalled the oppression he experienced and told his son that he would never go back to Cuba. Ted's mother, Elanor, graduated from Rice University with a degree in mathematics and became a computer programmer.

Ted Cruz has led the fight to defend life, marriage, the First and Second Amendments, and our entire Bill of Rights. Ted's wife, Heidi, and their two daughters, Caroline and Carol, feel blessed to live in America. Ted believes that Joe Biden's transcripts of him threatening to withhold money to Ukraine if they didn't fire their special prosecutor of corruption should be released. The transcripts of Joe Biden's dealings with China should also be released. Let the American people read the transcripts and decide.

In a brief but profound document titled "Human Fraternity for World Peace and Living Together," I endeavor to summarize its comprehensive content.

Page 1 declares that God created all human beings to respect and unite to foster harmony for the present and future generations. This lofty goal can be achieved by working together. We must recognize that multitudes of people are suffering, especially the poor and those dealing with social injustice, violence, and corruption.

Page 2 stresses that the wealthy have a moral obligation to help the poor improve their lives. The Catholics and Muslims must eschew policies and conduct that divide them; the document espouses dialogue between Catholics and Muslims to avert the destruction of the world's environment and climate.

Page 3 calls upon government leaders and religious leaders to promote peace, justice, and human fraternity. Insensitivity has led people to separate themselves. Hubris (pride) has caused people to withdraw from God to materialism! Lacking spiritual values, too often rich people exploit the poor for profit. Ungodly, super-rich people have the power to precipitate wars to make more money. The death and destitution of people, even children, is met with silence on the international level.

Page 4 decries the attack on children in the world by selfish people who do not care that poor children are not receiving education or a decent upbringing. The goal of all religions is to believe in God, a loving God. Government leaders must stop using religion to breed hatred, to justify war and violence. This is done to distract the common person from the real enemy.

The real enemy is the affluent elite who control the government and ignore the misery and plight of the poor.

Page 5 posits the teachings of Catholicism, which are rooted in the Bible, and the teachings of Islam, which are rooted in the Koran. These sacred scriptures teach tolerance and love for other people. We must augment religious awareness in young people to stave off selfishness, materialism, and greed. Freedom is a God-given right of every individual. The gender, race, and religion are willed by God in His infinite wisdom for every person. Ergo, a person cannot be subjugated to the will of another person. Justice based on compassion is the goal of Catholicism and Islam. It is incumbent upon the leaders of nations to address the economic, social, and political problems that affect the welfare of their citizens. The protection of synagogues, churches, and mosques of worshippers must be enforced by law. Terrorism must be eradicated, whether foreign or domestic.

Page 6 deems good relations between East and West as necessary for both. The West can learn from the East that materialism is toxic. The East can learn from the West essential science and technology. It is paramount to uphold human rights in the West and the East.

Gender discrimination has been curbed in the West. Women's rights are now being exerted in the East. It is necessary to protect females everywhere from male abuse. Women cannot be treated like property. Men cannot believe that a man is superior to a woman.

Page 7 proclaims the protection of children must be enforced vigorously by law. The protection of the rights of children must be sacrosanct, especially to receive good nutrition and education. The rights of the elderly and disabled must be enacted into law universally.

Pope Francis represented the Vatican, and the Grand Imam of al-Azhar is Ahamad Al-Tayyeb. These spiritual leaders will promulgate the "Document on Human Fraternity" to all schools, universities, and institutes of formation.

Friendship is what they hope to bring to fruition. We are all children of God, who has created us and loves us. These spiritual leaders presided over meetings held at Abu Dhabi in the United Arab Emirates on February 3–5, 2019.

Pope Francis is an ecumenical pope, as was Saint John Paul II. Pope Francis reflected on the Gospel of John (17:20–26) while meditating in the chapel of the Domus Sanctae Marthae on May 21, 2015. In particular, Pope Francis dwelled on Jesus's words "Father, I pray for these (apostles) but also for so many others who are yet to come." Saint Pope John Paul II sought unity among Christians. Pope Francis is seeking unity among all Christians, including Catholics, Protestants, Orthodox, Evangelicals, and Pentecostals. Pope Francis has a message that he delivered on video to all the leaders of the body of Christ, the Christian Church.

Yes, we have doctrinal differences, but the universal message is one: Jesus prayed for unity among us "as thou art in me, and I in thee." Christians must be united in love for one another because the devil is the father of division, of war, and envy even among Christian denominations. We have to be one as Jesus and His Father are one. We must not fight one another in war or be jealous of one another in things that work against unity in faith and love.

Pope Francis concluded his message for the "John 17" movement taking place worldwide: "We are capable of being witnesses of unity in the church and of joy in the hope of contemplating the glory of Jesus." In the first epistle of Saint John, the apostle, it is written in chapter 4, verse 16: "God is love and he that abides in love, abides in God, and God in him." Douay-Rheims is the Bible used for all these pages.

CHAPTER FOUR
China Will Rule the World

WHEN CHINA RULES THE WORLD BY MARTIN Jacquez and *Cracking the Apocalypse Code* by Gerard Bodson are the two secular sources I use in this chapter to fulfill Holy Bible prophecies. Here is a list of Chinese people murdered by their rulers over the past two thousand years: China's rulers include its citizens killed by emperors and the Chinese Communist Party dictator, Mao Zedong:

- An Lushan Rebellion (eight years)—twelve million people
- Xin Dynasty (fifteen years— twenty-two million people
- Ming Dynasty (seventeen years)—twenty-two million people
- Taiping Dynasty (fourteen years)—twenty million people
- Yuan Dynasty (thirty years)—twenty-five million people
- Mao Zedong (twenty-seven years)—forty million people

The Chinese emperors and the Chinese Communist Party (CCP) have murdered more than 140 million Chinese people. They are guilty of crimes against humanity. Do you think the Chinese Communist Party under Xi Jinping is fearful of starting nuclear WWIII in the near future? Xi Jinping suppressed dissent, exemplified by Hong Kong, Tibet, and the dentition camps for the Muslim Uyghur people. He had the fierce loyalty of the military. Hong Kong protestors have been crushed. Academics and intellectuals have been silenced; in fact, they endorse his hard line. Xi Jinping and the ninety million members of the Chinese Communist Party have complete control of the masses.

The tyrant of today's China seeks to surpass the United States in economic and military power, and the Holy Bible confirms that China will rule the world. Xi Jinping wants China to be the only superpower in the world. He is fond of repeating the words of the revered Chinese philosopher Confucius, who declared, "There can be only one sun in the sky." China will displace the United States as the superpower in the world. The Chinese nuclear forces grow in size and sophistication. China is secret about its nuclear forces but is aggressive in displaying its strategic intentions. China wants to control the southeast China Pacific seas and the southeast countries of Asia.

China is determined to quadruple its three hundred long-range nuclear weapons to equal the size of the United States and Russia. This will pose a nuclear threat to the United States and Russia. The Chinese have used Confucianism to support social hierarchy and autocratic rule. This is why China has supported Confucius institutes throughout the United States. The Chinese people are ecstatic about the election of Joe Biden as president because he is in the grip of left-wing socialists.

The COVID-19 virus originated in China, as did two of the devastating flu epidemics of the twentieth century—the Asian flu of 1957 and the Hong Kong flu of 1968, resulting in three million deaths worldwide. COVID-19 killed five hundred thousand Americans in 2020 and has caused more than two million deaths in the world. Could COVID-19 have been manufactured in the Wuhan laboratory and released on the world? There is no doubt in my mind that this virus was a major cause of Trump's defeat, much to the glee of the Chinese Communists. Is this virus the prelude to biological warfare? China's sphere of influence now extends throughout the world.

China exports its manufactured goods everywhere and imports the necessary raw materials from developing countries. China's tentacles stretch across East Asia, Central Asia, Latin America, and Africa since the start of its Road and Belt initiative a decade ago. Unlike the Asian Tigers like South Korea, Taiwan, and Vietnam, it has never been a vassal state of the United States. I believe the United States will one day be a vassal state, a tributary, perhaps an ally of China within the next twenty-five years. The United States has become a socialist state under the Democrats and may become a communist country by that time. Again, I urge my readers to read *Countdown to Socialism* by Devin Nunes.

The 1800s were dominated by European countries like France, Germany, and Spain but especially Great Britain. England prospered by the Industrial Revolution. The 1900s were dominated by the United States and its vast recourses, like coal and oil, and the great number of people. The population of the United States exploded in the twentieth century from immigration, especially from Europe. The population of the United States continues to expand today from immigrants from Central America and Mexico. The population of Hispanic people coming to the United States is now skyrocketing with no end in sight. China has never been a vassal state of Europe or the United States, not even when it endured the humiliation of the "Century of Humiliation" by these European countries and the United Stated, which lasted until the fall of the Qing Dynasty in 1912. The Chinese are a proud people with a four-thousand-year-old civilization. They are experts in trade and inventions, including gun powder, which changed the very nature of warfare. "Western hegemony is neither a product of nature nor is it eternal. On the contrary, at some point it will be to an end," as quoted in *When China Rules the World*. I posit that time has come for United States hegemony.

Communism is an ideology that holds that the ownership of property is by the community or a whole, not by the individuals. Communism is not practiced anywhere except by Catholic religious orders in monasteries, abbeys, convents, and so on. There are secular communities like the Amish or Mennonites that are Christian or the Hasidic Jews (ultraorthodox) that allow private property but share their financial resources to benefit their communities. Marxism is a political movement developed by Karl Marx and Fredrich Engels in the nineteenth century, based upon the theory that society inheritably develops through class struggle from oppression under capitalism to eventual classlessness. Chinese communism consists of state ownership of the means of production, combined with private ownership of business and real estate by individuals. However, all the citizens must pledge complete obedience to the Chinese Communist Party (CCP). There are ninety million members of this party, which allows about two million citizens to join the party annually. Members of the party become wealthier and work in factories or offices in the cities. The poorest people are farmers who live in the countryside. They must travel to the cities to work there with government-issued temporary work permits.

All people are required to attend school and become literate. However, to attend universities, high school students must pass rigorous exams, and the competition to go to college is fierce. All people in private companies and state-owned companies are educated. The entrepreneurs are also intellectuals who have traveled abroad and have been educated in the finest universities in Europe and the United States. They speak and write in English as well as Mandarin Chinese. They are the top echelon of society, living in fabulous luxury. All people in China have one thing in common: unquestioned loyalty to the Chinese Communist Party. Political activists, dissidents, human rights reformers, and more are eventually arrested and silenced.

Prosperity is the panacea. In 1980, more than 50 percent of the people lived in extreme poverty. In the rural villages, people lacked basic necessities, including electricity and running water. The lucky person owned a bike. In 2020, only 5 percent of the population lives below the poverty line. The transformation of agrarian to industrial China has been breathtaking. Credit for their accomplishments goes to the Chinese Communist Party. People will sacrifice personal freedoms when they are hungry. In the past, starvation from famines was commonplace. Under Mao Zedong, the masses endured the Great Leap Forward and the Cultural Revolution. The Great Leap Forward, based on collectivized farming, was a disaster. Millions died of starvation from famine induced by failed farming methods explored by the government. The Cultural Revolution precipitated the slaughter of landlords, landowners, and rich people. Students were encouraged to spy on everyone, even their parents. The value of being loyal to other people, even one's parents, was superseded by allegiance to the Communist Party. Professors were reeducated by working on farms. Yet Mao Zedong is revered in China because he established the Chinese Communist Party in 1949.

In 2021, Xi Jinping, president for life, controls the party and the people. This man is the most powerful person in the world, not Joe Biden. The United States is still a superpower, but China will be the number one superpower within twenty years. Recall the words of Confucius: "There cannot be two suns in the sky." From Deng Xiaoping to Hu Jintao, China enjoyed a peaceful and prosperous ascendancy, concentrated on growing the economy without making trouble with other countries, especially the United States. However, in the Deng and Hu era of amassing China's wealth without calling the attention of the world, Xi Jinping assumed the power of the presidency in 2012.

Xi Jinping was supposed to be president for ten years, until 2022. Instead, he named himself president for life. There was no dissent from the Chinese Communist Party. Xi Jinping was and is determined to make China the global powerhouse not only economically but militarily. He greatly expanded China's military. The Chinese built artificial islands in the South Pacific replete with a newer navy to tap this oil-rich area. Xi Jinping boldly proclaimed his dreams. He announced that China will become a global power second to none. In 2017, he announced China was building a powerful military. In 2018, he announced that "The Chinese people have the spirit of fighting the bloody battle against our enemies to the bitter end."

Europe and the United States are predicated on human rights, especially the rights of the individual. This is the antithesis of the Chinese ethos. The Chinese Communist Party denies human rights. All rights belong to the Chinese Communist Party. The human being has no God-given rights, such as life, liberty, and the pursuit of happiness. The Chinese Communist Party is atheist; there is no God.

On June 1, 2020, the *New York Times* published an article by Jimmy Lai, who is the chairman of the *Apple Daily* newspaper, the largest in Hong Kong. He wrote mainland China was opposed to Hong Kong's free people and free press. The Chinese Communist Party was determined to put an end to Hong Kong's protests. Jimmy Lai was arrested. Worldwide criticism stopped, and Hong Kong is firmly under the Chinese Communist Party control.

In 2043, China will attack Japan with nuclear weapons, starting nuclear WWIII and devastating Japan. The Chinese will never forget the Rape of Nanking, when the city was brutalized by the invading Japanese army. The United States will renege on its peace treaty with Japan to defend the country. China will achieve its vow to avenge the Chinese people.

By 2043, the United Socialist States of America and the resurrected Union of Socialist Republics will be allies of China. There will be no United Nations. China's authority will be observed throughout the world. All ethnicities, cultures, and religions will pledge allegiance to the People's Republic of China. Since the Democrats took over the presidency of the US as well as the Senate in 2020, they will control the future of our country. We will be a socialist county; our major corporations will be state run, and the banks and financial order will be run by the socialists. The wealth taxes on individuals will wipe out their wealth. Thus 50 percent of people who don't work will receive annual incomes from the heavy taxes of those who do work. Billionaires and millionaires will be among the 10 percent of all taxpayers who will shoulder the burden of funding the government. The Republican Party will be a shell of what it was since 2020. The Democrats will always have majority rule when they add four more senators from the newly stated Washington, DC, and Puerto Rico. Tens of millions of immigrants from Central American and Mexico will be granted citizenship and will vote Democrat. The US will be a country without a southern border. The immigrants will seek asylum, citing violence from drug cartels, and will be given amnesty and eventually citizenship.

Trump vs. China by Newt Gingrich is a sequel to *When China Rules the World* by Martin Jacques. There is no doubt in my mind that China will indeed rule the world during the Great Tribulation lasting seven years, starting in 2043 through 2050. The United States is trending toward socialism, especially among the youth. All Americans should read *The Case Against Socialism* by Rand Paul. China seeks to be the sole superpower in the next twenty years. Its economy and military are becoming the strongest in the world. The American socialists in power will make every concession that China demands.

Our country is presently a democracy. China is a totalitarian regime that plots to subjugate the world. China's symbol is the red dragon described in the Bible's book of Revelations. Xi Jinping is the antichrist who will start nuclear WWIII; if he dies before then, he has chosen his successor who will implement his plan. Xi Jinping has already begun biological warfare with the coronavirus, killing three million people worldwide. This Chinese virus has crippled the world's economies. The Chinese Communist Party has ninety million atheists who desire to eradicate all religions.

The Chinese have spies everywhere in America. Our universities are jammed with Chinese students on visas. They are taking advanced studies in technology, which they will use when they return to China. Students in China will never learn about the Great Leap Forward, the Cultural Revolution, and Tiananmen Square because the Chinese Communist Party will not allow these horrific events to be taught. The sad reality is that the left-wing professors in US colleges want these events to be shrouded in silence. Xi Jinping is emulating Mao Zedong in ruling China. He will allow no dissent and purge the rich and powerful who can collectively harm him. The Chinese military and masses adore him. They will worship him during the Great Tribulation beginning in 2043 and consider him to be god. If Xi Jinping dies before 2043, his successor will be declared by the Chinese Communist Party to be a reincarnation of Xi Jinping.

I cannot end this chapter without recommending the book *Firebrand* by Matt Gaetz. The book has nineteen chapters that are short and riveting. For my purposes, chapter 9 is precise in information concerning China. In thirteen pages, Matt explains and reveals why China is not our friend. While America has lost thousands of troops in Afghanistan and the Middle East and wasted trillions of dollars, China is bolstering its military, especially its navy with aircraft carriers.

Personally, I am elated that China has raised its population out of dire poverty. The Chinese people are industrious, working twelve hours a day in factories in the cities and on the farm in the country. Nobody should live in squalor and be denied the basic necessities of life. Everyone should have a decent education, going to college or vocational school. I admire the Chinese work ethic and discipline. Nonetheless, the Chinese Communist Party is an evil government determined to squash democratic reform and individual liberty. The CCP rules the Chinese people with an iron fist. The people must sacrifice their human rights and not think for themselves. The Chinese Communist Party is embedded in their psyche. China is a tragic case where the people are subject to mental and physical abuse, even death, by a dysfunctional government.

The Chinese Communist Party is likened to a giant trampling its own people. The people who live in the cities have material benefits. They live in high-rise condos with air-conditioning, exquisite furniture, wide-screen TVs, and so on. They have money to save in banks and invest in their stock markets. There has never been a time in China's history where so many people have been wealthy. They pay a huge price for these creature comforts. People are terrified by their government but will not voice their frustration. Their leader, Xi Jinping, speaks softly, with no blustering like Adolf Hitler, who mesmerized the German people with his fiery oratory, but he is shrewd and cunning. He manipulates his people like chess pieces. We must recognize this man as our mortal enemy bent on world conquest. Xi Jinping will start nuclear WWIII in 2043. Japan has no chance of retaliation without the United States mounting a nuclear attack on China in accordance with the peace treaty the United States signed with Japan to end WWII. We would not allow Japan to become an aggressor again.

By 2043, the United States will be a socialist country or even a communist country. The young people will have no will for combat with China. Better red than dead. Under the Democrats, we will go soft on China. This trend is already underway with the election victory of Joe Biden in 2020. A quote from *Fireland* written by Matt Gaetz: "Joe Biden is the classic China first American politician. The Biden Center at the University of Pennsylvania may have China connections that would make the Clinton Foundation blush."

I conclude chapter 4 with my personal experience with the Chinese Communist Party. In 1999, the CCP leader, Jiang Zemin, banned the Falun Gong in China. Since its inception in 1992 under Li Hongzhi, tens of millions Chinese people joined this spiritual faith. Of course, the CCP would not tolerate the Falun Gong and persecuted it as well as all religions in China. The

CCP continues to repress the Buddhists in Tibet, a conquered country. They burn Christian churches, which are not allowed to display crosses. They have even imprisoned a million Muslims, the Uighurs, in western China under the guise of reeducating them. Atheistic communism is determined to preclude man from being saved by a Creator. Karl Marx wrote that people's opium is religion and must be eradicated in his *Communist Manifesto*. There are one hundred million members of the Falun Gong, also called Falun Dafa, worldwide.

In the early nineties, I lived near a large community of Chinese residents in Flushing, New York. I joined the Falun Gong in peaceful protests in front of the main library on Maine Street and Northern Boulevard. The New York City police were present when a group of thugs armed with bats and chains attacked the protestors. The police defended us and made numerous arrests of these criminals. Unfortunately, some of the protestors were injured in the melee. A veteran police officer assured me that I would not be assaulted. He stood right in front of me.

With the protest over, a reporter from the *Epoch Times* asked me if I would like to be interviewed. I agreed and went to the office of the Falun Gong on Main Street in Flushing; I told them all that happened. They were grateful that I had participated in the peaceful protest. Then I was informed that the Chinese consul in New York City had hired the thugs that beat the protestors. The event was reported in the *Epoch Times*, and my interview aired on Tang Dynasty cable television.

If you want to know more about the ongoing persecution of the Falun Gong in China, read the book *How the Specter of Communism Is Ruling the World*, published by the *Epoch Times* newspaper. You will be aghast to learn that many Falun Gong practitioners in China are in prison and killed on demand, vivisected while still alive on the tables of state and military hospitals. Then their organs are sold for tens of thousands of dollars or even hundreds of thousands of dollars.

Notwithstanding this horrific reality, the movement is

flourishing. These people are like the early Christian martyrs in Pagan Rome. Recently, I read in the *Epoch Times*, a distinguished international weekly newspaper to which I subscribe, that the Falun Gong adherents and other prisoners of faith are being coerced to stop practicing their faiths. One heroine, Chen Yinghua, was being held in prison for refusing to give up her faith in Falun Gong. She was tortured by being denied sleep, not allowed to use the bathrooms or wash, coercing criminal inmates to choke her unconscious or beat her head against the walls. Finally, after four years in prison, she was released. Chen has relatives in the United States and Canada who pleaded for her release. The CCP did not want to be embarrassed by international exposure on the global stage and released her. We should all remember her warning words: "If people are not able to take action to resist and push back against the CCP, what the Chinese people are facing today will be everyone's tomorrow." (Jocelyn Neo and Arshdeep Sarao contributed to this report.)

When I completed reading the two volumes of *How the Spector of Communism Is Ruling the World*, I fully understood how Marxism's attacks on God, family, and traditional values are sweeping the world today. Our society is depraved since we have abandoned divinity with unbridled violence and lustful pleasures of the flesh. The worst instincts of humankind are exposed on television and the computer. The youth of the world is being ensnared by the devil. Most of what we see and read in the media is grotesque and bestial.

Our iniquity is greater than the days of Noah, and God will punish us with nuclear WWIII if we don't repent in a worldwide religious revival before the start of the Great Tribulation, a time of death and destruction that never was before: Isaiah 24:1, 3, 6; Matthew 24:21; Mark 13:19; and Revelation 12:12, "Woe to the earth and the sea, because the devil has come down to you, having great wrath, knowing that he has only a short time."

When communism took over China, the Chinese Catholics prayed the following prayer every day. Those who survived the mock trials of the communists attributed their release to the power of this prayer said daily.

> Oh my God, I fear only my fear; it could make me abandon thee.
> Oh my God, I fear only my fear; it could make me lose my courage before the end.
> Oh my God, do not forget me in thy glory, but give me thy love and the strength to give my life for Thee. Amen

Robert Gates, who was Barrack Obama's secretary of defense, asserted that the assumption that a richer China would be a free China was dead wrong. After forty years of economic growth, China is still a repressive regime.

China has the second largest economy in the world and will surpass the US in a matter of years. They are intent on becoming the sole superpower in the world. The Chinese Communist Party (CCP) tenaciously clings to the words of its ancient Chinese philosopher, Confucius: "There can only be one sun in the sky." The CCP boasts that it has made advances in science, technology, and artificial intelligence that now exceed the United States.

China has recently launched a hypersonic missile that could dodge the US missile defense system. The former national security adviser Robert O'Brien warned the Biden administration it could lose a war with China. In fact, Mike Gallagher, a Republican congressman, declared that China now has the power to launch a first-strike nuclear attack on us. China is rapidly increasing its number of nuclear weapons. It is now a threat to our national security. The present top general of the United States, Mark Milley, head of the Joint Chiefs of Staff, declaims that China has transformed itself both economically and militarily in the past forty years.

Today, China has intercontinental missiles capable of carrying nuclear warheads. We are witnessing the greatest shift in global geostrategic power that the world has ever witnessed. Furthermore, the United States is vulnerable to an attack from an electromagnetic pulse (EMP) that could wipe out our nation's power grid, killing millions of our population in a short time. An EMP is a burst of electromagnetic energy that disrupts communication and damages electronic equipment.

A high-altitude EMP could destroy 75 percent of US power generation capacity. Moreover, China has financially acquired cobalt from mines in the Democratic Republic of Congo in Africa. This country has two-thirds of the world's cobalt. Cobalt is necessary for the batteries of electric vehicles. China can produce forty thousand tons of cobalt, while the United States can produce six hundred tons of cobalt.

I began this chapter with the title "China Will Rule the World," and I end this chapter with the words China will rule the world.

CHAPTER FIVE

Holy Bible from the Ancient Eastern Text from the Aramaic of the Peshitta, Translated by George Lamsa and the Douay–Rheims Catholic Bible Listed in the Bibliography

THE QUOTATIONS FROM THIS HOLY BIBLE, the Ancient Eastern Text Aramaic of the Peshitta, may be found in any Christian Bible in circulation in English today. The only difference is that the author uses the word "China" throughout instead of "Gog." This Holy Bible differs from all other Bibles because it is based on Aramaic, the language that Jesus spoke. All other Bibles are translated from Hebrew, Greek, Latin, and other languages extant today.

In the first century, Jesus and His earliest believers certainly spoke Aramaic for the most part, although they also knew Hebrew.

Aramaic speech is an underlying fact that documents written in Aramaic were read by the writers of the New Testament. Aramaic was the language of the church that spread east from the beginning of Christianity, from Jerusalem and beyond the border of the Roman Empire. It is a miracle that Aramaic is still spoken in parts of Iraq and Iran, remnants of the Assyrian people and descendants of the Jews who were exiled. The Israelites never wrote their sacred scriptures but in Hebrew and Aramaic, which are sister languages. Greek was never the language of Palestine.

The Gospels, as well as the epistles, were written in Aramaic, the language of the Jewish people, both in Palestine and in the Greco-Roman Empire. *The Jewish Wars* written by the Jewish historian Josephus, was written in Aramaic in AD 42.

This is a direct quotation of George Lamsa, the biblical scholar who is the translator of this Bible: "All the English speaking in Asia will welcome a translation based on what they believe to be pure original sources which have been carefully kept all these centuries without the slightest modification or revision. I firmly believe that this work will strengthen the faith in Jesus Christ of many Christians in the Near East and the Far East and enhance missionary efforts in spreading The Word of God to millions of people in Asia. These were the facts which motivated me when I undertook this task, to which I have devoted my life."

Nota bene: All other Christian and Jewish Bibles use the words *Gog* and *Magog* to refer to "eastern" and "northern" tribes. The Holy Bible in Aramaic Peshitta specifically pinpoints the "eastern tribes" as China!

It is my honor to quote some scripture verses from the Holy Bibles. Please note carefully that the word *Gog*, which appears in modern Catholic and Protestant Bibles, has been translated into the word *China* by the biblical scholar George Lamsa. This reinforces my steadfast belief that China will start nuclear WWIII in 2043 and rule the world for seven years until the second coming of Jesus Christ.

"Behold the Lord shall destroy the earth and lay it waste and turn it upside down and scatter its inhabitants" (Isaiah 24:1 Douay–Rheims).

"The land shall be utterly destroyed and utterly spoiled; for the Lord has spoken this word" (Isaiah 24:3 Douay–Rheims).

"Therefore, the earth shall sit in mourning, and all its inhabitants shall be condemned; therefore all the inhabitants of the earth shall be destroyed, and a few men shall be left" (Isaiah 24:6 Douay–Rheims).

What a horrific description of the Great Tribulation in the New Testament (Matthew 24:21). What a horrific description of nuclear WWIII (Douay–Rheims).

"Son of man, set your face against China and against the land of Mongolia, the chief prince of Meshech and Tubal" (Ezekiel 38:1, 2 Aramaic Peshitta).

"Therefore, son of man, prophecy and say to China, thus says the Lord God: On that day when my people Israel shall dwell in tranquility and you shall know it" (Ezekiel 38:14 Aramaic Peshitta).

"And it shall come to pass at the same time when China shall come against the land of Israel, says the Lord God, that my anger be consumed in my fury and zeal" (Ezekiel 38:18 Aramaic Peshitta).

"I will subdue you and father you together, and I will course you to come up from the north parts, and bring you upon the mountains of Israel" (Ezekiel 39:2 Douay–Rheims).

China will attack Israel with its allies from the north. Josephus, the eminent Jewish historian, identifies Meshech and Tubal as the land of the Scythians as Magog, now occupied by Russia. The armies of China and Russia and Persia and Turkey will attack. Persia (now Iran) and Gomer (now Turkey) will join the invasion.

"And it shall come to pass on that day I will give to China a place there for burial in the land of Israel, the great valley which is east of the sea; and they (Israel) shall close off the valley and there they shall bury China and all his army; and it shall be called the valley of the annihilation of China" (Ezekiel 39:11 Aramaic Peshitta).

Troops of China and its allies will number two hundred million (Revelation 9:16 Douay–Rheims).

"For them there will be great suffering such as has never happened from the beginning of the world until now, and will never be again" (Matthew 24:21 Douay–Rheims).

"Then the sign of the son of man will appear in the sky, and all the generations of the earth will mourn, and they will see the son of man coming on the clouds of the sky with power and great glory" (Matthew 24:30 Douay–Rheims).

"And he will send his angels with a large trumpet, and they will gather his chosen ones from the four winds, from one end to the heaven to the other" (Matthew 24:31 Douay–Rheims).

"For in those days there will be suffering such as has never been the beginning of the creation which God made until now, and never will be again" (Mark 13:20 Douay–Rheims).

"Then they will see the son of man coming in the clouds, with a great army and with glory" (Mark 13:26 Douay–Rheims).

"And I saw an angel come down from heaven, having the key of the bottomless pit (hell) and a great chain in his hand. And he seized the dragon (the dragon is the symbol of China), that old serpent, which is the tempter and Satan, who deceived the whole world, and bound him for a thousand years" (Revelation 20:1, 2 Douay–Rheims).

"And when the thousand years come to an end, Satan shall be loosed from out of his prison, and shall go out to deceive the four corners of the earth, even to China and Mongolia, to gather them for war; the number of them is as the sand of the se." (Revelation 20:7, 8 Aramaic Peshitta).

"I testify to every man who hears the words of the prophecy of this book, if any man shall add to these things, God shall add to him the plagues that are written in this book; and if any man shall take away from the words of this book of this prophecy, God shall take away from portion from the tree of life and from the holy city and from the things which are written in this book! He who testifies these things says, surely I am coming soon. Amen. Come, Lord Jesus. The grace of our Lord Jesus Christ be with you all, all you holy ones. Amen" (Revelation 22:18–21 Douay–Rheims).

All Christian Bibles confirm the coming of the Great Tribulation, which will end in seven years, the second coming of Christ, and the establishment of the millennial kingdom, ruled by Jesus Christ. Jesus will destroy Satan and his evildoers in the battle of Armageddon after His reign on earth for one thousand years. He will then ascend to heaven with all the saved people for all eternity. The Holy Bible from the Ancient Eastern Text is invaluable and unique. George Lamsa has identified China as the greatest threat to humanity in his translation of the Holy Bible from the Aramaic Peshitta (simple, sincere), the language that Jesus spoke to His apostles and the earliest disciples. I am an Ecumenical Catholic. I have the utmost respect for my Protestant brethren. They know by heart the Holy Bible, especially the Baptists and Evangelicals, rejoicing in a personal born-again relationship with Jesus. These Christians fully realize the importance of daily Bible readings. The zeitgeist of the twenty-first century is that we are all God's children loved by God: "God is love, and he who abides in love abides in God, and God lives in him" (1 John 4:16 Douay–Rheims).

I agree with my Protestant brothers and sisters in a literal interpretation of the millennial kingdom, ruled by Him, and lasting one thousand years.

"And so all Israel shall be saved" (Romans 11:26 Douay–Rheims). When the armies of China, Russia, and Iran are poised to invade Israel after the Great Tribulation (nuclear WWIII), Jesus and his army of angels will return to defeat them and save all Israel.

"I will make you a light to the nations, that my salvation may reach to the ends of the earth" (Isaiah 19:6 Douay–Rheims). When Jesus returns to earth, Israel will be a light to the nations since Jesus will establish his kingdom in Israel for one thousand years during the millennial kingdom.

All the world will know that He is the messiah. "Woe to the earth and the sea, because the devil has come down to you, having great wrath, knowing that he has only a short time" (Revelation 12:12 Douay–Rheims). Satan is on a rampage. Global war, crime, drugs, and immorality emanate from the evil one and his human cohorts. These are the last days. Satan knows that very soon Jesus will return to earth to vanquish him; Satan and all evildoers will be cast into hell, where the fire is not extinguished.

The wage of sin is death (Romans 6:23 Douay–Rheims). War is a consequence of sinfulness. Nuclear WWIII is on the way if we don't repent of our grave iniquity. Our wickedness today is as great as in the days of Noah and Sodom and Gomorrah. If we do not repent, we will perish. "For the days are coming declares the Lord, when I will restore the fortunes of my people Israel and Judah." The Lord says, I will them back to land I gave to their fore-fathers, and they shall possess it" (Jeremiah 30:3 Douay–Rheims). This end-time prophecy was fulfilled with the establishment of Israel in 1948 and the full restoration of Jerusalem and the Golan Heights in 2020 by President Donald Trump when he moved the American embassy to Jerusalem from Tel Aviv.

"And it shall be the days, God says, that I pour forth the spirit upon all mankind; and your sons and your daughters shall prophesy, and your young men shall see visions, and your old men will dream dreams" (Acts 2:17 Douay–Rheims). I am one of those men; I will prophesy until I die.

"So it will be at the end of the age, the angels will come forth, separate the wicked from the just and cast them into the furnace of fire. There will be gnashing of teeth" (Matthew 13:49, 50 Douay–Rheims). The end of the age is when Jesus returns to earth with His host of angels to wage the battle of Armageddon.

The righteous people will be spared, while Satan and his demons and evildoers will be cast into hell. God is just.

"For them there will be a great tribulation, such as not occurred since the beginning of the world until now, nor ever shall" (Matthew 24:21 Douay–Rheims).

I believe the Great Tribulation will be nuclear WWIII, starting with a nuclear attack on Japan by atheist communist China in 2043. This event is foretold by Gerard Bodson and a team of computer scientists in *Cracking the Apocalypse Code* (Element Books, 2000). They arrived at this date through the use of gematria—that is, number symbolisms in Hebrew. Each letter of the Jewish alphabet has a numerical equivalent. Two thousand forty-three was waiting in the last book of the Bible, Revelation, to be discovered by means of the computer. Gerard Bodson is a theologian and scholar. His team collaborated to discern the prophecies of Revelation to discover the genesis of Armageddon. The team of Gerard Bodson consisted of Myriam, a Jewish theologian speaking fluent Hebrew and versed in gematria, Jean-Pierre, a semiologist, and Dimitri, a historian. This team collaborated with Father Alexander, a Greek monk from the Mount Athos monastery. This erudite group calculated the year 2043 as the beginning of the Great Tribulation when diabolical China attacks Japan with nuclear weapons. The United States (unless an ally of China by then) is bound by treaty to defend Japan. We will counterattack China with nuclear missiles. Thus commences nuclear holocaust, which will become worldwide since these countries have alliances with numerous nations.

"And the word of the Lord came to be saying, son of man set your face against China and against Persians (Iran), and the uttermost parts of the north (Russia), and many other people who are with you. Therefore, son of man prophesy and say to China, thus says the Lord God: On that day when my people Israel shall live in tranquility, you shall know it" (Ezekiel 38:1–14 Aramaic Peshitta).

This translation was made by George Lamsa, estimable Bible

scholar, from the Aramaic Peshitta, the Holy Bible from the Ancient Eastern Text (HarperOne, an imprint of HarperCollins Publishers, 1968). Magog was identified by Josephus as the land of the Scythians now occupied by Russia. China and its allies will be poised to invade Israel after the seven-year Great Tribulation (2043–2050).

Jesus will return to earth (we do not know the date; only God the Father knows.) Jesus will vanquish Satan, his demons, and all evildoers and cast them into hell. Thus, Israel will be saved from destruction, and all its Jews will accept Jesus as their messiah.

"Satan will come out to deceive the nations which are in the four corners of the earth, Gog and Magog, to gather together for war; The number of them is like the sand of the seashore. And the number of the armies was two hundred million" (Revelation 20:8 and 9:16 Douay–Rheims). Gog (China) and Magog (China's allies) will rapidly muster two hundred million troops to invade Israel from the east and the north, but they will be annihilated by Jesus and His army of angels, led by St. Michael the archangel, prince of this heavenly host.

When China Rules the World (Penguin Press, 2009) is authored by Martin Jacques, noted historian and writing professor at Renmin University in Beijing. It is projected that the economic and military hegemony of Europe and the United States will be eclipsed by China in the near future. Today, China has the second largest economy in the world. By 2027, China will surpass the United States as the world's largest economy. The Chinese Communist Party and the populace are strengthening their military forces with nationalistic fervor. The Chinese despise the Japanese for their invasion of China in WWII and the barbaric Rape of Nanking. Babies were tossed into the air and bayonetted by Japanese soldiers.

China will soon settle the score with Japan. In the nineteenth century, Europe was the dominant power in the world. In the twentieth century, the power shifted to the United States. In the twenty-first century, China will achieve superiority in a new global order. China has the largest population in the world, one and a half billion people, ruled by the ruthless, malevolent Chinese Communist Party. From the ranks of its numbers, ninety million strong, has emerged its dictatorial leader, Xi Jinping, the president for life. He or his successor, chosen by him, will be the antichrist prophesied by Hebrew and Christian scriptures (Daniel, Matthew, 2 Thessalonians, 1 John, and Revelation Douay–Rheims). The dragon is the symbol of Satan. The dragon is the symbol of China. All the emperors of China had the dragon displayed on their flags.

Now I would like to include other Bible verses contained in the Holy Bible from the Douay–Rheims that confirm we gain salvation through Jesus Christ. When we die, He will judge us with one criterion. Have we been loving or unloving?

"I am the way, the truth and the life, no one comes to the Father, except through me" (John 14:6 Douay–Rheims).

"For God so loved the world that He gave His only begotten son, so that whoever believes in Him should not perish, but live eternal life" (John 3:16 Douay–Rheims).

"So that they all may be one; just as thou, my Father, art with me and I am with thee, so that they may be one with us; so that the world may believe that thou didst send me" (John 17:21 Douay–Rheims).

"He who believes. In him would not be condemned; and he who does not believe has already been condemned for not belief in the name of the only begotten son of God" (John 3:18 Douay–Rheims).

"He who believes in the son has eternal life; and he who does not obey the son shall not see life, but the wrath of God shall remain on him" (John 3:16 Douay–Rheims).

"And they said to him, believe in our Lord Jesus Christ, and both you and your household will be saved" (Acts 16:31 Douay–Rheims).

"Truly, truly, I say to you, the time is coming, and it is already here, when the dead will hear from the son of God; and those who hear it, will surely live" (John 5:25 Douay–Rheims).

"And this is the testimony, that God has given to us eternal life, and this life is in his son. He who believes in the son has life; he who does not believe in the son of God does not have life" (1 John 4:16 Douay–Rheims).

"For we are his creation, created through Jesus Christ ultimately for good works, and God has ordained that we live in them" (Ephesians 2:10 Douay–Rheims).

"Jesus said to her, I am the resurrection and the life; he who believes in me, even though he die, he shall live. And whoever is alive and believes in me shall never die. Do you believe this?" (John 11:25, 26 Douay–Rheims).

The Books of the Old Testament

At this juncture, I will attempt to do something daring. I am going to select quotations from the Douay–Rheims Catholic Bible cited in the bibliography and point out their relevance to Donald Trump. Dear reader, see if you agree or disagree with my response. My beloved wife, Phyllis, urged me to connect the dots between the Bible and Donald Trump.

Bear in mind, there are thirty-nine books of the Old Testament and twenty-nine books of the New Testament in this Bible. If you don't agree with my response, by all means, formulate a response of your own.

Douay–Rheims, Genesis 1:28, "And God blessed them, and God said to them, be fruitful and multiple, and fill the earth and subdue it."

My response: Donald Trump has certainly complied with God's behest.

Douay–Rheims, Exodus 24:20, "Behold, I send an angel before you to guard you on the way and to bring you into the land which I have prepared."

My response: Donald Trump has been assigned an angel by God to guide him to lead the United States.

Douay–Rheims, Leviticus: 4:27, "And if any one of the common people of the land sin through ignorance, while he does something against any of the commandants of the Lord concerning things which ought not be done, and be guilty."

My response: The Democrats accused Donald Trump of things that were not true. They accused Trump of collusion with Russia, obstruction of justice, and incitement of insurrection.

Douay–Rheims, Numbers 6:3, "He shall abstain from wine and strong drink."

My response: Donald Trump does not drink wine or liquor.

Douay–Rheims, Deuteronomy 23:24, "When you come into your neighbor's vineyard you may eat grapes, you fill at your own pleasure; but you shall not put any into your vessel."

My response: Donald Trump may eat grapes, but he does not drink wine.

Douay–Rheims, Joshua 1:9. "Behold, I have commanded you. Be strong and of good courage; fear not neither be dismayed; for the Lord your God is with you wherever you go."

My response: Donald Trump is strong, courageous, and not dismayed because God is with him.

Douay–Rheims, Judges 5:9, "My heart said to the forgiven of Israel, they are chosen among the people bless the Lord."

My response: Donald Trump worked with Netanyahu, former leader of Israel.

Douay–Rheims, Ruth 4:13, "So Boaz took Ruth, and she became his wife; and when he went into her, the Lord gave her conception and she bore a son."

My response: Donald married Melania, and she bore a son named Barron.

Douay–Rheims, 1 Samuel 2:2, "There is none holy like the Lord; for there is none besides thee; and there is none powerful like our Lord."

My response: needless to say, Donald Trump is not holy or powerful as is God.

Douay–Rheims, 2 Samuel 5:1, "Then all the tribes of Israel

came to David at Hebron and said to him we are your flesh and your bone."

My response: it would have been wonderful if all Americans felt this way about Donald Trump when he was their president.

Douay–Rheims, 1 Kings 3:28, "And all Israel heard the judgment which the king of judged; and they feared the king; for they knew that the wisdom of God was in him, to do justice."

My response: Corrupt politicians and bureaucrats fear Donald Trump because they know he is a wise man who will do justice to them. That is why they don't want him in public office.

Douay–Rheims, 2 Kings 18:6, "For he held fast to the Lord and turned not a side from following him, but kept his commandments, according to all that the Lord commanded Moses."

My response: Donald Trump is a good Christian who obeys the Ten Commandments.

Douay–Rheims, 1 Chronicles 4:10, "The Lord shall surely bless and enlarge your territory, and His hand shall be with you and shall deliver you from evil, that it may have no power over you, and shall grant your requests of him."

My response: Donald Trump has acquired much real estate all over the world.

Douay–Rheims, 2 Chronicles 1:8, "And Solomon said to the Lord, thou has shown great mercy to David my father, and hast made me to reign in his stead."

My response: Donald inherited a fortune in real estate when his father died.

Douay–Rheims, Ezra 1:2, "Thus says Cyrus King of Persia: The Lord God of Heaven has given me all the kingdoms of the earth, and he has commanded me to build him a house in Jerusalem, which city is in Judah."

My response: In the past, Persia (today Iran) wanted to help the Jews build a temple in Jerusalem. Today, Iranian leaders want to destroy Israel. Under Donald Trump, the United States was Israel's close ally.

Douay–Rheims, Nehemiah 11:2, "And the people blessed all the men who willingly offer themselves to dwell in Jerusalem."

My response: When Donald Trump moved the American embassy from Tel Aviv to Jerusalem, this was a sign that Jerusalem would be the capital of Israel forever.

Douay–Rheims, Esther 1:20, "All wives shall give honor to their husbands, both great and small."

My response: Melania Trump has given honor to Donald Trump since their marriage in 2005.

Douay–Rheims, Job 5:7, "For man has been born for trouble, as sure as the wild birds fly."

My response: The Democrats have tormented Donald Trump unjustly.

Douay–Rheims, Psalm 23:4, "Yea, though I walk through the valley of the shadow of death, I will fear no evil; for thou art with me; thy rod and thy staff will comfort me."

My response: Donald Trump was not assassinated in his first term of office as president, nor will he be assassinated in his second term of office as president.

Douay–Rheims, Proverbs 19:14, "House and riches are the inheritance from father; but a wife is betrothed to a man from the Lord."

My response: Donald inherited much wealth from his father, but Melania is a gift from the Lord.

Douay–Rheims, Ecclesiastes 5:18, "This what I, the Preacher have seen: It is good and comely for one to eat and drink and to enjoy the good of all his labor for which he toils under the sun all the days of his life, which the Lord has given him; for this is his portion."

My response: I believe Donald Trump has worked hard in his campaign to become president and worked very hard to improve the lives of all Americans.

Douay–Rheims, Solomon 1:2, "Let him kiss me with the kisses of his mouth; for your love is better than wine."

My response: Melania prefers the kisses of her husband more than sharing some wine.

Douay–Rheims, Isaiah 24:1, "Behold, the Lord shall destroy the earth and turn it upside down and scatter its inhabitants."

My response: this is the grim prophecy of Isaiah alluding to the Great Tribulation, which is forthcoming nuclear WWIII if we reject God.

Douay–Rheims, Jeremiah 1:5, "Before I formed you in the belly I knew you; and before you came out of the womb I sanctified you and ordained you a prophet to the nations."

My response: God had a plan for Jeremiah, Donald Trump, and each one of us before we were born. God detests abortion. God is pro-life.

Douay–Rheims, Lamentations of Jeremiah 1:7, "Jerusalem remembers in the days of her affliction and of her chastisement all her pleasant things that she had in the days of old. When her people fell into the hand of the oppressor and she had none to help her, her oppressors saw her, and mocked at her destruction."

My response: Jeremiah prophesied the destruction of Jerusalem by Babylonia in 586 BC and then by Rome in AD 70 because the Jews had turned their backs to God and committed evil. In the days of old, under King Solomon, they were righteous and became powerful and prosperous. In 1948, the Jews returned to Israel, after being dispersed throughout the world, the Diaspora. At present, things look positive for peace between Israel and their Arab neighbors. The Abraham Accords were initiated by President Donald Trump. However, with the emergence of China, Israel's future is in doubt. China's intent is to rule the world, including Israel.

Aramaic Peshitta, Ezekiel 39:11, "And it shall come to pass on the day that I will give to China a place there for buried in the land of Israel, the great valley which is east of the sea; and they shall close off the valley; and there they shall bury China and all his army; and it shall be called the valley of the annihilation of China."

My response: within the next twenty-two years, China will build the greatest military in the world. In 2043, China will begin the Great Tribulation by attacking Japan with nuclear missiles, devastating Japan. The United States, much weaker than China, will renege on its treaty to defend Japan, which was signed when Japan surrendered to the United States, ending WWII. Thus, China will avenge its invasion by Japan during WWII. During the Great Tribulation, which lasts seven years, China will subdue the world through diplomacy and/or nuclear war. China will break its peace treaty with Israel and attempt to invade Israel with vast numbers of troops. Israel cannot win a nuclear war with China. God will not allow China to conquer Israel. The son of God, Jesus Christ, and His host of angels will slay the vast Chinese army.

The Great Tribulation is over. Jesus will set up His millennial kingdom, which reigns on earth in peace and prosperity for one thousand years. Jesus will rule from Jerusalem.

Douay–Rheims, Daniel 12:1, "And at that time shall Michael arise, the great angel who has charge over your people; and shall be a time of trouble such as never been like it since the beginning of the world; and at the same time some of your people will be delivered, everyone whose name shall be found written in the book."

My response: The prophet Daniel was given a vision of the last days when China will attempt to invade Israel, but its army will be vanquished by Jesus and St. Michael the archangel. Every Jew whose name is found in the Book of Life will be spared from death, but all evildoers will die along with the atheist Chinese troops.

Douay–Rheims, Hosea 1:10, "Yet the number of the children of Israel shall be as the sand of the sea, which cannot be measured nor numbered and it shall come to pass that in the place where it was said to them, you are not my people; there it shall be said to them, you are the sons of the living God."

My response: Today, the number of Jews is about twelve million, a quarter of 1 percent of the world's population. During the millennium the number of Jews will increase greatly.

Douay–Rheims, Joel 1:20, "But Judah shall dwell forever and Jerusalem from generation to generation."

My response: Israel and Jerusalem are in God's hands forever.

Douay–Rheims, Amos 9:14, "And I will back the captivity of my people Israel, and they shall build the ruined cities and inhabit them; and they shall plant vineyards and drink the wine thereof; they shall also plant gardens and eat the fruit of them."

My response: When the Jews returned to Israel and were granted statehood in 1948, they immediately began to restore the land that had been neglected by the Ottoman Empire. They built irrigation canals and grew vegetables. In short, they made the desert bloom. They established new settlements called kibbutzim. The Jews sought peace with the Arabs who attacked them when they were granted a homeland. Statehood is still an option for the Palestinians, but Jerusalem will never be divided again. This is not an option; no east Jerusalem under Arab control.

Douay–Rheims, Obadiah 1:15, "For the day of the Lord is near upon all nations; as you have done, it will be done to you; your rewards shall be done to you."

My response: Atheist Chinese Communist Party, beware! When your troops attempt to invade Israel, they will be destroyed by Jesus Christ and a host of angels.

Douay–Rheims, Jonah 3:5, "So the people of Nineveh believed in God and decreed a fast and put on sackcloth, from the greatest of them even to the least."

My response: When Jonah warned the city to repent of its evil ways, the people did so. God forgave them and spared this great city from destruction.

Douay–Rheims, Micah 6:8, "He has showed you, O man, what is good and what the Lord requires of you, that you shall do justice and have mercy and be ready to walk after the Lord your God."

My response: Donald Trump is a just and compassionate man. He follows God's commandments. This is a message for all of you.

Douay–Rheims, Nahum 1, "The Lord is slow to anger and great in power, and will not acquit the wicked; the Lord's way is in the tempest, and the clouds are the dust of his feet."

My response: The Lord is patient with the wicked, but if they don't repent and change their evil ways, He will punish them. This is a message for all people.

Douay–Rheims, Habakkuk 2:7, "Behold, they shall rise up suddenly, those who shall bite you, and awake, those who shall cause you trouble, and you shall be spoil to them."

My response: The Democrats seized on the opportunity to vote by mail due to the pandemic. Voting by mail and harvesting ballots, extending voting past the deadline, not requiring valid signatures, counting votes of dead people, and changing rules for election during the election—all these devious tactics cost Donald Trump the 2020 election.

Douay–Rheims, Zephaniah 3:18, "I shall remove from you those who spoke reproach against you."

My response: all the people who accused Donald Trump of collusion with Russia, obstruction of justice, and inciting an insurrection will lose their jobs when Trump is elected president in 2024.

Douay–Rheims, Haggai 2:5, "According to the covenant which I made with you when you came out of Egypt so my spirit remains among you; fear not."

My response: as long as Israel obeys the covenant God made with Moses, Israel will flourish among the nations.

Douay–Rheims, Zechariah 8:9, "For the seed shall be prosperous; the vine shall give its fruit and the ground shall yield its increase and the heavens shall give their dew; and I will cause the remnant of these people to possess all these things."

My response: When the Jews regained their homeland, Israel, in 1948, the barren desert was made to bloom, and Israel became a powerful, progressive nation in the Middle East. Donald Trump was raised by God to move the American embassy from Tel Aviv to Jerusalem and implement peace treaties with the Arabs.

Douay–Rheims, Malachi 1:11, "For from the rising of the sun even to its going down, my name is great among the Gentiles; and in every place they burn incense and offer to my name pure offerings; for my name is great among the Gentiles, says the Lord of Hosts."

My response: monotheism was introduced to the world by the Jews; belief in one God spread to the pagans through Christianity and Islam.

The Books of the New Testament

Douay–Rheims, Matthew 24:4, "For then there will great suffering such as never happened from the beginning of the world until now, and never will be again."

My response: In *Cracking the Apocalypse Code* by Gerard Bodson, China will attack Japan with nuclear weapons in 2043. The islands will be devastated entirely. China will rule the world by then. No one wins in nuclear WWIII, so the hegemon China makes the rules for the world through the diplomacy of the Chinese Communist Party, making treaties with all nations, with the threat of nuclear war holocaust. China accomplishes its goal of world domination in seven years. This period of time is called the Great Tribulation. China will demand tributes or threaten war. China will make a peace treaty with Israel but will break it after three and a half years. China's leader will order the Jews to worship him as a god. Israel will refuse and prepare for an invasion by China.

Douay–Rheims, Mark 13:19, "For in those days there will be suffering such as has never been from the beginning of the creation which God made until now, and never will be again."

My response: The apostles Matthew and Mark have made identical prophecies. China's leader is the antichrist. He will initially allow the Jews to rebuild the temple in Jerusalem, but after three and a half years, he will desecrate the temple by demanding the Jews to worship him as a god! Xi Jinping is president of China today, ruling the country with an iron grip.

He will choose his successor, who is described in Revelation as the antichrist. Human beings will have a mark on them, probably inserted as a chip in their bodies. If anyone refuses this mark, he or she will not be allowed to buy or sell anything. This person will die of starvation. In the Bible, the sign of the beast, antichrist, is the number 666. Donald Trump will probably be dead by 2043, but if he is still alive, he will certainly not worship the antichrist or receive his sign. He is a true Christian!

Douay–Rheims, Luke 6:45, "A good man brings out good things from the good treasures of his heart; and a bad man from the bad treasure of his heart brings out bad things; for from the abundance of the lips speak."

My response: The crowds filled the stadiums for Donald Trump. They listened to him because he spoke from his heart, not from a script. Donald Trump boasted that the United States is the greatest country in the world. He vowed to drain the swamp of crooked politicians and bureaucrats in Washington, DC. He did his best to bring back manufacturers who left the United States because of high taxes on their companies. Donald Trump improved the income of all Americans through lower payroll taxes. Donald Trump was not a career politician but a successful businessman who cared about Americans and wanted them to live better. That's why seventy-five million Americans admired him, myself included. That's why he will win another term as president in 2024.

Douay–Rheims, John 15:4, "Remain with me and I with you. Just as a branch cannot give fruit by itself unless it remains in the vine even so you cannot unless you remain with me."

My response: All supporters of Donald Trump must remain loyal to him. Individually, we cannot stop the United States from becoming a socialist one. Under the Biden administration, the federal government will take control of our lives, stripping away our freedom of religion, free speech, right to assemble, and right to bear arms. The federal government, especially the executive branch that is the presidency, and the legislative branch will be under the control of the Democrat Party. This is the goal of the left-wing, radical Democrats—to crush the opposition, the Republican Party. All socialist and communist countries have one political party. The hope of Republicans is to beat the Democrats at the ballot box in 2022 and 2024. Registered Republicans must remain loyal to Donald Trump and other Republican office holders, except for the RINOs.

Douay–Rheims, Acts of the Apostles 19:40, "For even now we are in danger of being charged with sedition, for we cannot give an answer concerning this day's meeting, because we have assembled for no reason, and have been tumultuous without a cause."

My response: On January 6, 2021 Donald Trump held a rally outside the Capitol. He addressed his supporters with just cause. There was evidence of voter fraud in the November election. Republican Senators were providing the Senate with evidence of voter fraud that denied him the presidency. Donald Trump had every legal right to protect the election results.

He urged his supporters to voice their protest peacefully— certainly not to invade the Capitol and disrupt the proceedings. Nonetheless, the House of Representatives majority Democrats voted to impeach him for inciting insurrection. A mock trial was held in the Senate even though he was out of office at the time and the Supreme Court chief justice was not presiding over the sham trial. Of course, he was acquitted and has the legal right to run for the presidency again in 2024.

Douay–Rheims, the epistle of Paul the apostle to the Romans 1:16, "For I am not ashamed of the gospel of Christ; for it is the power of God to salvation to everyone who believes, whether they are Jews first and also to the Greek."

My response: Jesus preached the gospel to the Jews, the lost sheep of Israel. Jesus commissioned his disciples to preach the gospel to all nations. If a person knows the gospel to be true but then rejects it, that person is lost to salvation. However, if a person does not know the gospel, he or she can be saved by being a loving person. This person loves the God of his understanding through the faith he or she has been taught by the elders. Thus, non-Christians may be saved because their ignorance of the gospel is not culpable. They have the baptism of desire to know the truth of the gospel.

Douay–Rheims, the first epistle of Paul the apostle to the Corinthians 1:10, "How I beseech you, my brethren, in the name of the Lord Jesus Christ to be of one accord, and let there be no divisions among you but be perfectly united in one mind and in one thought."

My response: Doctrinal differences between Catholics and Protestants have perpetuated hostility and even warfare among them in the past. Thank God, the bloodshed has ended. We have much more in common in the teachings of Jesus Christ than the differences in the teachings of his disciples of varied denominations. In the past, there was hatred among Christians, whether Catholic or Protestants or Orthodox. Jesus does not want it to be this way. Faith in Jesus should unite all Christians in love, not enmity. Faith in Jesus, love of Jesus, cannot be divisive.

Douay–Rheims, the second epistle of Paul the apostle to the Corinthians 7:4, "I am familiar enough to speak boldly with you, and I am very proud of you; I am filled with satisfaction, and I am overwhelmed with joy in all our troubles."

My response: Indeed Donald Trump is very proud of his followers, notwithstanding the folly of several hundred who invaded the Capitol, ignoring his plea for a legal, peaceful protest. Donald Trump is not distressed about losing the election. He is overjoyed by the loyalty of his Republican base. After five weeks in office, Joe Biden has issued excessive executive orders detrimental to the oil, natural gas, and coal industries. Already, gasoline prices have increased markedly, and summer traveling hasn't begun. An open border with Mexico is displeasing millions of Americans, Democrats and Republicans. A soft approach to China will enrage them. The leftists dread the 2022 and 2024 elections. RINOs, your Republican constituents will not forget your treachery in these forthcoming elections.

Douay–Rheims, the epistle of Paul the apostle to the Galatians 5:14, "For the whole law is fulfilled in one saying, that is you shall love your neighbor as yourself."

My response: Albeit a billionaire, Donald Trump is not an elitist. He is a populist; every American is considered a neighbor. That's why he can fill the stadiums with people chanting, "We love you." He is not a politician; nor does he speak like one. He speaks from his heart, not the polished script of a political speech-writer. Donald Trump wants manufactured goods to be made in America, not in China, as has been the case for the past thirty years. He is a tough negotiator in trade deals with China. That's why the Chinese were jubilant when he lost the election. Donald Trump cares about the poor. African Americans and Hispanics had the highest levels of employment that they had ever had under any president before him. They rewarded him with more votes than the Democrats expected. Donald Trump loves America, its democracy and capitalist economy. Socialism will result in tyranny. Rand Paul made a cogent argument in his book *The Case against Socialism*, which should be read by every American. Joe Biden and his left-wing comrades will wreck our economy with their fantasy $50 trillion Green New Deal. The Democrats will tax the middle class to death with their alternative energy nonsense. No restraints on fossil fuel carbon emissions for China and India with their three billion people. Joe Biden has rejoined the Paris Climate Agreement, which will continue to pollute the planet.

Douay–Rheims, the epistle of Paul the apostle to the Ephesians 2:10, "For we are his creation, created through Jesus Christ ultimately for good works, and God has before ordained that we should live in them."

My response: All people were created to love others and to do good works. Donald Trump and Joe Biden have this in common; however, Satan and evil spirits prowl the earth like hungry lions, to ruin our souls. We must resist the devil through love of God and other people. This is the reason we were created by God.

Douay–Rheims, the epistle of Paul the apostle to the

Philippians 1:28, "And that in nothing are you terrified by our adversaries, whose conduct is the sign of their own destruction, but your salvation, and this is from God."

My response: The left-wing progressives, socialists, and communists are atheists. These godless people want to foist their will on the majority of Americans who are religious and conservative. These left-wing people in politics, Hollywood celebrities, and CEOs, especially Big Tech and fake media moguls, are hateful immoral people who hate people who practice their religions, whether it be Judaism, Christianity, or Islam. These evil people are leftist Democrats. They sense there is a huge, youthful movement to the right. The Democrats have the slimmest majority in the House in more than a hundred years, just five seats. They are evenly split in Congress and have a hypocritical president who calls himself Catholic but permits babies to be murdered one minute before their births. One minute before they are born! They passed a $1.9 trillion COVID-19 bill in the House, with only 9 percent going directly to care for the China virus victims. It is glaringly evident that the Democrats, under Joe Biden, are self-destructing. Five weeks on the job, he has issued executive orders to lay off workers, especially blue-collar workers, in the oil, natural gas, and coal industries. Magically, they are supposed to find work in technology. Most of the COVID-19 bill will be used to bail out bankrupt cities and states run by the Democrats. One hundred fifty billion dollars goes to education, not to benefit students who have not been in school but to the strong teachers' unions whose teachers are demanding big salary raises while the schools are closed for nearly a year.

The Republicans will take back Congress in 2022, and President Trump will win by a landslide in 2024. The Democrats know they are in big trouble.

Douay–Rheims, the epistle of Paul the apostle to the Colossians 1:10, "That you might live a righteous life, please God with all good works, and bring forth good fruits and grow in the knowledge of God."

My response: The Democrats charged Donald Trump with collusion with Russia, obstruction of justice, and incitement of insurrection. They impeached him twice, even after he was out of office. They tried to destroy a righteous man. They failed miserably.

Douay–Rheims, the first epistle of Paul the apostle to the Thessalonians 3:7, "Therefore, our brethren, we have been comforted by you, in the midst of all our distress and tribulations because of your faith."

My response: Donald Trump takes comfort in the support of his fans. Through all the malicious attacks on him, he knows we have faith in him.

Douay–Rheims, the second epistle of Paul the apostle to the Thessalonians 1:11, "Therefore, we always pray for you, that God will vouchsafe you worthy of your calling and satisfy all your desires, which are for goodness and the works of faith with power."

My response: Many Republicans, especially the Evangelicals, believe that Donald Trump was raised by God to thwart the progressives, socialists, and communists who hate this country and its Constitution. These people are atheists who yearn to ban freedom of religion and all our rights enshrined in our Bill of Rights. They will do anything to gain power. The government is their god. These evil people endeavor to brainwash the public with their poisonous propaganda.

Douay–Rheims, the first epistle of Paul the apostle to Timothy 1:4, "Now the fulfillment of the commandment is love out of pure heart and of a good conscience and of a true faith."

My response: We are all sinners! Donald Trump may have been lustful and greedy in the past. When we are young, the pride of life can be overwhelming. But Donald Trump is a righteous man today. His wife, Melania, is a graceful woman. Donald Trump loves her; she has been a shining example of love of God and caring for others. I am sure he has a good conscience and faith in God, being married to her these past fifteen years.

Douay–Rheims, the second epistle of Paul the apostle to

Timothy 1:7, "For God has not given us a spirit of fear but of power and love and of good discipline."

My response: This verse is a perfect description of the personal attributes of Donald Trump. He is not fearful of the politicians, Democrats or RINOs, who seek to crush him. They never will succeed in their nefarious deeds because Donald Trump is one of the most powerful, loving, and disciplined presidents with whom the United States has been blessed. He has been called by God to save our country, the home of the free and the brave, from wretched people hell-bent on making our democracy a socialist, tyrannical government. Donald Trump sought to stop this country from decline and ruin by making America great again. Donald Trump loves America and all its people regardless of race or religion. He has demonstrated his love of its people by his policies, which have given its citizens greater opportunities to make higher incomes and improve their lives. He supports the military and police strongly to defend us from foreign enemies and domestic criminals. The populace will thank Donald Trump by reelecting him as president in 2024.

Douay–Rheims, the epistle of Paul to Titus 3:8, "This is true saying, and these things I want you to constantly affirm so that those who believe in God may be careful to do good works continually. These things are good and profitable to men."

My response: We are justified by faith in God. It was God who ordered Abraham to sacrifice his son, Isaac, as a holy holocaust. It was not good works but faith in God and obedience to God that engendered the Abraham Covenant, by which God blessed Abraham with many descendants who were Jews and ultimately blessed many nations of Gentiles. If one truly believes in God, that person will then perform many good works. You are saved by your faith in God.

Douay–Rheims, the epistle of Paul to Philemon, verse 6, "That the participation of your faith may bear fruits in works, and in knowledge of everything that is good which you have in Jesus Christ."

My response: Paul's epistle to Titus is immediately followed and confirmed by his epistle to Philemon. Everything good is in Jesus. Jesus said, "I am the way, the truth and the life, no one comes to the Father except through me." Jesus will judge us when we die. He decides who goes to heaven or hell (John 14:6).

Douay–Rheims, the epistle of Paul to the Hebrews 1:3, "For he is the brightness of his glory and the express image of his being, upholding all things by the power of his word; and when he had through his person cleansed, our sins, then he sat down on the right hand of the majesty on high."

My response: Jesus Christ is the Son of God—begotten, not made, and consubstantial with the Father. Jesus has two natures: divine and human. He was like us, human, in all things save sin. He was crucified, died, and was raised from the dead on the third day. He spent forty days with His apostles in His glorified body. Then He ascended to heaven, where He sits at the right hand of His father. He will return to earth to judge the living and the dead. He will establish and rule a temporal kingdom for one thousand years, the millennium. During the millennium, Christ will reign on this earth (Isaiah 2, 3; Daniel 7:14; Zechariah 14:9). Satan will not be free to work (Revelation 20:2). Righteous will flourish (Isaiah 11:33). Peace will be universal (Isaiah 2:4).

The productivity of the earth will be greatly increased (Isaiah 35:1–2). At the conclusion of the time. Satan will be loosed to make one final attempt to overthrow Christ but without success (Revelation 20:7–9). Source: *The Ryrie Bible Study* by Charles Caldwell Ryrie, ThD, PhD. Satan will be "loosed a little season" (Revelation 20:1–3) so that he can harvest souls of the people who reject Jesus during the millennium. Remember, the people alive during the one thousand years will still have free will to accept or reject Jesus as their savior and Son of God. They will be able to sin even though Satan is bound in hell during the millennium. "He who is unjust will continue to be unjust, and he who is filthy will continue to be filthy, and he who is righteous, will continue to do righteousness and he who is holy will continue to be holy" (Revelation 20:11).

Douay–Rheims, the general epistle of James 2:24, "You see then how a man by works becomes righteous, and not by faith only."

My response: Actions speak louder than words. A person who says he is Christian but does not act like Jesus is not a disciple of Jesus. Jesus wants us to help someone in need. If the person is hungry, feed them. If the person is thirsty, give them a drink. You need faith with good works; otherwise, your faith is dead. "Was not our father Abraham justified by works, when he raised Isaac his son upon the altar? You can see how his faith helps his works, and by his works his faith was made perfect" (verses 21–22).

Douay–Rheims, the first epistle general of Peter: "Blessed be God, the Father of our Lord Jesus Christ, who by his abundant mercy has again renewed us spiritually to a lively hope by the resurrection of Jesus Christ from the dead."

My response: If Jesus did not rise on the third day, there would be no Christianity today. If Jesus did not rise with a glorified body and spend forty days on earth with His apostles, and if He had not been seen by more than five hundred believers, there would be no Christianity today.

Douay–Rheims, the second epistle general of Peter, "But, my beloved, do not forget this one thing, that one day in with the Lord a thousand years, and a thousand years as a day."

My response: The skeptics will say Jesus promised to return to earth from heaven more than two thousand years ago. So where is He? I will answer that two thousand years is like two days to God. Jesus may tarry, but He will not be late. He is giving sinners more time to repent. God is slow to anger, but his patience with habitual sinners is not infinite. We are living in a time of immorality and violence more than in the times of Noah. We are living in the last days of this social order. When Jesus returns, he will destroy our civilization and decimate humanity. Satan, his demons, and evil people will be cast into hell. Our God is merciful but just. We will be chastised severely!

Douay–Rheims, the first epistle of John 2:9, "He who says he is in the light but hates his brother is therefore in darkness even until now."

My response: "God is love and he abides in love and he who dwells in love abides in God" (1 John 4:16). We have known the love God has for us.

Douay–Rheims, the second epistle of John, verse 6, "For this is love, that we walk according to his commandments. This is the commandment that you heard from the beginning, you should follow it."

My response: "Whoever trespasses and does not abide in the teaching of Christ does not love God. He who abides in his doctrine has both the Father and the Son" (verse 9).

Douay–Rheims, the third epistle of John, verse 11, "Our beloved, do not follow that which is evil, but that which is good. He who does good is of God; but he who does evil has not seen God."

My response: President Donald Trump has done much good for our country. He has never done anything evil against our country. We were blessed by God to have him as president of our country for one term. I pray God he has a second term!

Douay–Rheims, the general epistle of Jude, verse 20, "But you my beloved, build upon yourselves anew, the holy faith through the Holy Spirit, by means of prayer."

My response: I firmly believe in the power of prayer. With God, all things are possible. People of all faiths should pray that all human beings everywhere repent of all their sins and turn to God for forgiveness. I hope that the book *The Coming of the Great Awakening* by Mike Evans engenders a religious revival throughout the world. We must pray that the Holy Spirit will stir the souls of the spiritually dead to have faith in God.

Lax non-Christians' faith in God will be restored. All people will accept Jesus Christ as the Son of God and their personal Savior. "With God all things are possible" (Matthew 19:26).

Douay–Rheims, the revelation of Saint John the Divine, "And

when the thousand years come to an end, Satan shall be loosed out of his prison" (Revelation 20:7).

My response: When the thousand years of the millennium are over, Satan will emerge to wage war with Jesus Christ again. China and other nations will be defeated at the battle of Armageddon once and for all. "Fire came down from heaven and consumed them" (Revelation 20:9). "And the devil who deceived them was cast into the lake of fire and brimstone and shall be tormented day and night forever and ever" (Revelation 20:10).

Repentance is one of the most crucial themes in The Old Testament and The New Testament.

Douay–Rheims, Psalm 34:14, "Depart from evil and do good; seek peace and pursuit it."

Douay–Rheims, Isaiah: 55:7, "Let the sinner forsake his way, and the wicked man his thoughts; and let him return to the Lord, and he will have mercy on him; and to our God, for he will abundantly pardon."

Douay–Rheims, Luke: 24:47, "And that repentance should be preached in his name for the forgiveness of sin among all nations; and the beginning will be from Jerusalem."

Douay–Rheims, Acts: 26:20, "But I preached first then of Damascus and then at Jerusalem and throughout the village of Judaea and then to the Gentiles, that they might repent and turn to God and works worthy of repentance."

Remember, if people across the world beg God for the forgiveness of their sins, if people repent of their violence and immorality, then God will spare us the Great Tribulation—that is, nuclear WWIII. The Lord wants us to love one another, not hate one another. We must do good, not evil. God spared Nineveh, a great city, when its people repented of their wickedness and turned to Him. Teshuva, however, time is running out; our ingenuity is as great as it was in the days of Noah. God decimated humanity with a great flood of water. If we don't repent now, we will very soon be destroyed by nuclear fire.

There is one scripture and quotation from the Holy Bible from the Ancient Eastern Text from the Aramaic of the Peshitta that does not refer to China but to Japan: "And I will send a fire in Magog, and on the people who dwell peacefully in the islands; and they shall know that I am the Lord." A footnote identifies Japan as the peaceful islands (Ezekiel 39:6).

China will devastate Japan with nuclear weapons in 2043 in revenge for the Rape of Nanking during WWII. Bear in mind that the Great Tribulation (nuclear WWIII) commences in 2043, lasting seven years. This fact is confirmed in a secular source: *Breaking the Apocalypse Code* by Gerard Bodson, included in the bibliography.

The coronavirus has yielded unprecedented powers to politicians. Many elected officials are selecting what businesses and organizations may operate. Some are telling you whether you can eat in a restaurant, go to your gym or hair salon, and attend church and school. They even seek to regulate the number of friends and loved ones that you may entertain in your own home.

Power-hungry politicians, such as New York Governor Andrew Cuomo and Mayor Bill de Blasio, revel in making regulations. In fact, they are eager to arrest hardworking people who do not follow the Left's oppressive rules. The manager at Mac's Public House on Staten Island was apprehended in a December raid for failing to follow Governor Cuomo's COVID-19 restrictions related to a 10:00 p.m. tavern curfew. The pushback demonstrates the growing frustration people have with government overreach. In California, a backlash has occurred over COVID lockdowns. While small restaurants were being told they could not have outdoor dining, Hollywood movie sets were permitted to hold large catered events. Though health risks are real and Americans must remain responsible, the California government is complicating matters by dictating hypocritical rules, such as forbidding outdoor dining.

All over, small businesses are being targeted and hurt by

radical shutdown policies, while malls stay open. If small businesses dare to operate outside of the tight restrictions to survive, they must bear the burden of oppression or be punished for going against regulations. Time to let your representatives know that Americans will no longer tolerate mass constraints against folks who are desperately trying to keep their business going, provide a roof over their heads, and feed their families.

Ben Ferguson is host of the fastest growing conservative podcast in the country "Ben Ferguson Podcast." Download it now! *AMAC* magazine.

EPILOGUE

Dear Readers,

Bear in mind, the Chinese Communist Party is ninety million strong, including all its card-carrying members. It is under the complete control of the antichrist, Xi Jinping. The CCP is persecuting all people who have faith in God. The members of the CCP are avowed atheists who hate Chinese Christians and Muslims, who are monotheists. The CCP despises the Falun Gong since these people acknowledge divinity (God) and evil (Satan). The bulk of Chinese people are righteous and spiritual; they are not demon possessed as are members of the CCP. There are more than a billion Chinese people in China and around the world who desire to destroy Marxism.

The Marxist Chinese have unleashed the coronavirus and its variants on the world. This is recorded in all Christian Bibles: "And I heard a great voice saying to the seven angels, go your way and pour out your seven bowls of the wrath of God upon the earth" (Revelation 16:1).

These bowls of the wrath of God are the plagues that the CCP is spreading around the world, killing four million people, including more than 960,000 Americans.

The coming Great Tribulation (Nuclear WWIII) commences in 2043 when China destroys Japan, as recorded in all Christian

Bibles: "Behold, the Lord shall destroy the earth and turn it upside down and scatter its people. Therefore, all the earth shall be destroyed and a few men shall be left" (Isaiah 24:1, 6 Douay–Rheims). "And I will send a fire on the people who dwell peacefully in the islands" (Japan) (Ezekiel 39:6 Aramaic Peshitta). China will devastate Japan in revenge for the Japanese invasion of Japan and Rape of Nanking in WWII.

The world has twenty-two years left to repent of its egregious sins, get on its knees to beg for forgiveness, and await the return of Jesus Christ.

> I testify to every man who hears the words of the prophesy of this book, if any man shall add to these things, God shall add to him the plagues that are written in this book; and if any man shall take away the words of the book of this prophesy, God will take away his portion of the Tree of Life and from the holy city and from the things which are written in this book. He who testifies these things says, surely I am coming, coming soon. Amen. Come, Lord Jesus. The grace of our Lord Jesus Christ be with you all, all of you holy ones. Amen. (Revelation 22:18, 19, 20, 21 Douay–Rheims)

Warning!

Do you want your children and grandchildren to live in a communist country like Cuba, North Korea, or China? Republicans, Democrats, and Independents, unite now to save the United States of America from becoming a communist country.

I prophesy that if the world does not repent of its iniquity, turning to God and away from sin, in the next twenty-one years, the Great Tribulation (nuclear WWIII) will commence in 2043 when communist China attacks and destroys Japan with nuclear weapons. The United States will renege on its peace treaty with Japan since old religious conservatives like myself will be dead by then. The majority of young people will have no will to defend Japan. They will be depraved communists, addicted to drugs and sexual promiscuity, and godless.

The Great Tribulation will be short-lived, only seven years, but the Chinese Communist Party—all atheists—will rule the world under the successor of Xi Jinping, the antichrist! Mirabile dictu! The Second Coming! Jesus Christ will return to earth to establish His temporal kingdom, casting Satan and his demons to hell for one thousand years—the millennium!

Satan will be loosed from hell for a short time. The evil one will master a military of two hundred million diabolical troops who will wage the battle of Armageddon in Israel. They will be devoured by fire, which will come down from heaven. Finally, Jesus will judge the souls of these damned souls and multitudes of others from the Great White Throne in the New Jerusalem. All righteous people on earth will ascend to heaven, which is the New Jerusalem for all eternity.

Promise!

My beloved and always hopeful wife, Phyllis, urged me to close our book with optimism. We must pray for a miracle! If many people all over the world repent, turning to God and away from evil, our all-loving and merciful God will spare us from the Great Tribulation, nuclear WWIII. When the people of Nineveh heeded the prophet Jonah and repented of their wickedness, God spared their city from destruction. God changed His mind for them and will do the same for us. I promise you!

BIBLIOGRAPHY

Bodson, Gerard. *Cracking the Apocalypse Code*. Boston, MA: Element Books, Inc., 2000.

Chumley, Cheryl. *Socialist Don't Sleep*. West Palm Beach, FL: Humanix Books, 2021.

Dobbs, Lou. *The Trump Century*. New York, NY: Harper Collins Books, 2020.

Fitton, John. *A Republic Under Assault*. New York, NY: Simon and Schuster, 2020.

Gaetz, Matt. *Firebrand*. Nashville, Tennessee: Post Hill Press, 2020.

Gingrich, Newt. *Trump VS China*. New York, NY: Hachette Books, 2019.

Hannity, Sean. *Live Free or Die*. New York, NY: Simon and Shuster, 2020.

Haydock, Rev. George Leo. *Douay-Rheims*. Pekin, Indiana: Gatley Company Refuge of Sinners Publishing, Inc, 1883.

Horowitz, David. *Dark Agenda*. West Palm Beach, FL: Humanix Books, 2020.

Jacques, Martin. *When China Rules the World*. New York, NY: Penquin Books, 2009.

Lamsa George. *Holy Bible from the Ancient Eastern Text*. New York, NY: Harper Collins Books, 1933.

Levin, Mark. *Unfreedom of the Press*. New York, NY: Simon and Schuster, 2019.

Loudon, Trevor. *The Enemies Within*. Salem, Oregon: Pacific Freedom Foundation, 2013.

Nunez, Devin. *Countdown to Socialism*. New York, NY: Encounter Books, 2020.

Paul, Rand. *The Case Against Socialism*. New York, NY: Harper Collins Publishers, 2020.

Shapiro, Ben. *How to Destroy America in Three Easy Steps*. New York, NY: Harper Collins Publishers, 2020.

Strang, Stephen, *God and Donald Trump*. Lake Mary, FL: Frontline Publishers, 2017.

Ward, Jonathan. *China's Vision of Victory*. Arlington, VA: The Atlas Publishing and Media Com, LLC, 2019.

Wei, Lingling and Davis, Bob. *Superpower Showdown*. New York, NY: Harper Collins Publisher, 2020.